W9-BKG-693

WITHDRAWN

6/06

I.C.C. LIBRARY

WITHDRAWN

Composition in Convergence

The Impact of New Media on Writing Assessment

Composition in Convergence

The Impact of New Media on Writing Assessment

I.C.C. LIBRARY

Diane Penrod
Rowan University

LAWRENCE ERLBAUM ASSOCIATES, PUBLISHERS
2005   Mahwah, New Jersey   London

PE
1404
.P386
2005

Copyright © 2005 by Lawrence Erlbaum Associates, Inc.
All rights reserved. No part of this book may be repro-
duced in any form, by photostat, microform, retrieval
system, or any other means, without prior written permission of the publisher.

Lawrence Erlbaum Associates, Inc., Publishers
10 Industrial Avenue
Mahwah, New Jersey 07430
www.erlbaum.com

Cover design by Kathryn Houghtaling Lacey

Library of Congress Cataloging-in-Publication Data

Penrod, Diane.
   Composition in convergence : the impact of new media on
   writing assessment / Diane Penrod.
       p. cm.
   Includes bibliographical references and index.
ISBN 0-8058-4590-9 (alk. paper)
ISBN 0-8058-4591-7 (pbk. : alk. paper)
   1. English language—Rhetoric—Study and teaching. 2.
English language—Rhetoric—Study and teaching—
Technological innovations. 3. English language—Rheto-
ric—Study and teaching—Data processing   4. Report
writing—Study and teaching (Higher)—Technological in-
novations.   5. Report writing—Study and teaching
(Higher)—Data processing. 6. Online data processing—
Authorship—Study and teaching. 7. Grading and mark-
ing (Students). 8. College prose—Evaluation.   I. Title.

PE1404.P386 2005
808'.042'0285—dc22   2004056418
                                                                    CIP

Books published by Lawrence Erlbaum Associates are printed
on acid-free paper, and their bindings are chosen for strength
and durability.

Printed in the United States of America
10 9 8 7 6 5 4 3 2 1

To Frank
and the "big fluffy puppies," Koan and Kuma,
and to my students

Contents

Preface

About the time I started researching the connections between computer technology and writing assessment in earnest, Dennis Baron's essay in *The Chronicle of Higher Education* appeared (November 20, 1998, p. A56). Baron's observations that essay-grading software packages based on predicate analysis or keyword in context algorithms would somehow streamline faculty grading processes and make those processes more consistent (i.e., efficient) seemed as on target then as they do today, 5 years later.

What has changed in the last 5 years, though, is the continual merging of computer technology and writing assessment in the composition classroom. This merging of technology is called "convergence" in media fields, and the idea of convergence is incredibly appropriate for what happens in the writing classroom. In convergence, more than simple blending takes place; often, a re-visioning or reconceptualizing of practices and products occurs. For Composition, convergence offers writing teachers a way to redefine literacy through the electronic text, or e-text. The e-text can span many genres: blogs, MOOs, web pages, e-mail exchanges, text messages, and so on. E-textual writing requires instructors to reconceptualize both the text and the criteria under which the text can be evaluated. Consequently, as the product changes, the practices underlying the creation of these new products should change as well. So too should we expect a change in the practices for evaluating electronic texts beyond layering holistic scoring models, analytic rubrics, or portfolio assessment onto the work. Convergence has brought the field to the era that Kathleen Blake Yancey described as the "fourth wave" in writing assessment (1999).

In the pages that follow, I try to understand what Yancey's fourth wave in writing assessment looks like. How does this new phase in assessment differ from older periods in terms of historical significance, textual characteristics, student ownership of the text, validity and reliability, teacher practices, and access to important technologies? Important shifts occur in these areas as the two technologies in Composition— computers and writing assessment—play an increasingly more important role in the teaching of writing. Moreover, there is much for writing instructors and their programs to discuss and discover in the convergence process, because it appears as though different institutions will enter and resist these new contexts at various stages. We need to see convergence in Composition not just as a global phenomenon that affects the entire field but as a succession of liminal moments that ebb and flow over time. Convergence is also a highly localized happening as well in that each institution's political, social, economic, and cultural forces will shape the way the technologies are blended. What looks right in a research-based university may not fit a 2-year college or a comprehensive state university.

That is why the material presented in these chapters is not as prescriptively written as some readers may have liked. Although I do offer suggestions and ideas based on what has worked in my classrooms over the last few years, that information should be taken solely as suggestion and idea generation. If studying convergence has taught me one thing, it is that anything written as being "the way" to implement instruction using technology will be outdated by the time the book is published. Technology moves at a much more rapid pace than publication. That is why I hope my work is used as fodder for discussion, consideration, and improvement on what has been presented to date. There are many ways to work with the convergence of technologies in the writing classroom; each of us has to seek out what works best for us, our students, and our programs. Perhaps there are talented graduate students or junior faculty who can take this material, improve on what has been written, and lead the field into the next waves of technological convergence. I certainly hope so.

To return to Dennis Baron's 1998 essay: Regardless of the levels of convergence that emerge in Composition, Baron is right: None of us—neither students nor teachers—should forget our day jobs when it comes to technology and writing. Writing is a significant aspect of the learning process. It demonstrates how and why we think the way we do; it should challenge us to see the world and our thoughts differently when we complete an assignment; it should help us discover more about the relationships we have in our studies and in our lives. If technology leads us toward better, more thoughtful writing, then that is a good thing. If we let technology supplant writing in the Composition classroom, then our day jobs are in danger.

I wish to thank many people for helping me discover more about the relation that exist between computer and assessment technologies in the writing classroom. First, there are the scholars cited throughout this book. Their ideas, theories, and suggestions made me look long and hard at what was happening in my own classroom. Second, my students are central to what transpired over the last 5 years. Their interest in, resistance to, and enjoyment of computers and writing assessment made it clear to me that faculty need to pay attention to how technology affects the entire learning process. Last, thanks to Linda Bathgate, my editor, and Karen Wittig Bates, my assistant editor, at Lawrence Erlbaum Associates, for believing in this book. Each of these relationships has been important in its own respect. Although all these individuals played a significant part in the development of this project, any errors or omissions are mine alone.

Glassboro, New Jersey
July 2004

About the Author

Diane Penrod is professor of composition and rhetoric at Rowan University, Glassboro, New Jersey. She is site director for the National Writing Project at Rowan University and graduate program coordinator for the master of arts in writing. She teaches undergraduate and graduate courses in evaluating and assessing writing, writing with technology, information architecture, and qualitative and quantitative research methods. Her current research focuses on the influence and function of trust in the college writing classroom. Diane is also developing an essay collection with a group of teachers in Grades 7 through 12 that centers on teaching popular culture at the secondary level.

Introduction: Composition at the Crossroads of Convergence: What Happens When Technologies Intersect in Pedagogical Spaces?

Writing has always been aligned with technology, from the ancient scratchings on cave walls to the present tapping of keystrokes on a laptop. Technology, as media scholar Lawrence Grossberg defined it, connects us to tangible means of making, remaking, and distributing commodities, services, materials, and cultural products (Grossberg, Wartella, & Whitney, 1998). Writing also connects us to these same areas, because many commodities, services, materials, and cultural products depend on the written word in some way.

Like technology, writing is not an unconstrained part of society—both are molded and managed by various social organizations, such as education and government, which make particular decisions regarding production and use. Writing and technology, then, share several important characteristics and tensions heightened by the arrival of the computer age: communication, power, mediation, and determination. Each of these aspects has particular roles as Composition undergoes its latest convergence with technology in pedagogical spaces.

With regard to communication, the rise of computer technology in the writing classroom has moved writing beyond a closed academic exercise. Computer-based classroom writing has emerged as a form of public discourse, with all the attendant variations of opinions, values, skills, abilities, interests, and desires that follow. As electronic genres like "blogging" blossom in the writing classroom experience, issues of legitimation and power over language certainly emerge. Instructors and students struggle over who "owns" the electronically produced classroom text, and such issues and tensions require mediation to provide a successful learning environment. Last, determination in this new pedagogical realm needs consideration. Determination is not simply instructors and students having the fortitude to handle heretofore unimaginable difficulties with computer malfunctions or software glitches. Rather, determination in this new writing situation includes how these technologies influence, control, and govern how faculty and their programs construct pedagogical goals and values related to all aspects of writing instruction. This determination includes how writing assessment enters into the context for learning and how students respond to evaluation. The role of how writing assessment influences, controls, and governs curricula is becoming increasingly important in higher education. As the technologies inherent in writing assessment come together with computer technologies in the writing classroom space, various tensions emerge and reemerge.

This book attempts to explore what these tensions are as writing assessment and computer technology converge on classroom space. However, I can make no promises that this examination of the issues can resolve the tensions. Perhaps no amount of study can resolve the tensions that exist. The difficulties span political, economic, philosophical, and pedagogical spectra. What I hope to offer with this book is the opportunity for teachers to engage with each other and with their administrations regarding how local issues, tensions, and concerns might be addressed.

Clearly the rise in demand for both computer technology and assessment technology ushers in significant pedagogical changes for colleges and universities. As with any critical shift in education, alarmist rhetoric is sure to be offered by many—whether triggered by the opposition or by concerned allies. Currently, instructors see this sort of rhetoric in the mounting calls for accountability on college campuses, the charges of lax standards in college-level writing, and the suggestions that perhaps computers can "read" student essays better and more efficiently than professors can.

Many accusations circulate about the drop in standards surrounding student literacy. Societal factors—family income, social status, family stability, gender, race, and geography—blend with institutional pressures and the move toward a more electronic media-based culture. These elements also contribute to shifts in literacy and the notion of standards. Still, the computer does seem to shape writing practices, habits, and outcomes, which can lead critics and some supporters to overdetermine the effects computers have on writing. Assessment often helps push these findings, because the mediating qualities of writing assessment generally assume a clear, objective understanding of what good writing is, and what the corresponding standards are, despite the context in which the writing is produced. If the criteria for good writing are grounded in fixed, print-based notions, then any mediation process will favor that position and will continue to promote both reactionary discourse and oversimplified understandings of what computers can do for student writing and for evaluation. However, when probed more deeply, many of these contentious challenges wax nostalgic or moral in substance. Little sound pedagogical information related to teaching writing or studying the habitual practices of writers connects to the discussion. Nonetheless, in these times of rabid and rampant demands for accountability in education nostalgic and moral arguments frequently hold greater public and institutional sway than one might expect.

For the last 15 or so years, though, the growth of communication technologies, the emphasis on writing in the classroom, the beginnings of rearticulating writing assessment for the classroom, and the works of several composition scholars, researchers, and technorhetoricians have made significant inroads regarding moving the field to the point where I can write that technological convergence has created a crossroads in Composition. This point most everyone freely acknowledges, despite his or her pedagogical position.

Convergence—the blending of several technologies into a single source—has affected the teaching of writing in ways that few could have imagined 30, 60, or 100 years ago. The present vehicle for convergence in Composition, the computer, speeds up the demand and the production of text-based knowledge, and that old journalism saw, "Get it fast, but get it right," which has been broadened to "Get it fast, get it right, get it immediately," now extends to the expectations readers have for online texts. This is a major change from the thoughtful, time-infused *belles lettres* understanding of writing that shapes how many teachers were trained and the ideas they pass on to their students. Reflection and insight may be critical components for academic writing, but for most networked writing situations, information and content are central. Students have to write quickly and well in this brave new world.

Other pedagogical changes have occurred as well. No longer does strict process theory hold for writing instruction in a Composition affected by technology. Today's faculty face teaching writing in a "postprocess" mode, a place where computers make written work public and situate one's language in various uncontrollable contexts and discourse settings. Computers also allow for the production of seamless texts. In these contexts, writing becomes highly collaborative, as writers rapidly share ideas across their screens, and so the communicative acts of writing often surpass the strictly academic performances expected under traditional forms of assessment. In return, each of these influences places pressure on what students and their instructors view as information and knowledge—as well as what "good writing" is—in the classroom and how student achievement is measured when a class is asked to construct new information and knowledge in an electronically rich environment.

Given our culture's experiences with technology, Composition must grapple with technology's effects on writing and writing instruction. Americans will not slow their demand for quick information and knowledge. If anything, writing faculty should anticipate the public's increased expectations for electronic texts to become more available and the standards for quality raised higher while increasing the speed with which the information is transferred. These demands are not just for the academic or student writer, either. The use of electronic texts and increased electronic textual production will occur for the nonacademic writer as well, especially as more middle and lower income American families gain affordable access to smaller, powerful computers and peripherals, Internet services, and text messaging services (Alter, 1999; Rheingold, 2002). Our students face a present and a future where careers depend heavily on both strong writing skills and rapid information transfer.

Compared to 10, 15, or 20 years ago, greater numbers of writing specialists understand the advantages that exist when students compose in networked spaces, and even more now recognize the advances that digital technologies have made in writing instruction and pedagogical theory that benefit critical thinking in a complex society. Some teachers realize the incredible creativity, imagination, and interactivity that writing assignments can have in cyberspace, and that realization grows yearly as more instructors turn to hybridized or fully computer-based composition in the writing classroom. Most faculty have web pages, and many teach with programs like WebCT, NiceNet, or BlackBoard for all or part of their courses.

There is, though, one area of writing instruction that is now being emphasized in networked spaces: assessment. Until recently, perhaps the last 2 or 3 years, in Composition there was a lack of sustained inquiry regarding whether and how these two technologies can be successfully blended. The condition facing writing teachers is one in which computer technology sufficiently alters both a writer's knowledge base and the definition of what is a text to such a degree that fundamental writing assessment methods and terminology no longer apply. Although the traditional language and ideas driving writing assessment seem retrograde when compared with what compositionists do in the computer-based classroom, these assessment practices remain. The language, criteria, and ideas are ported from paper to pixel even though one technology calls the other into question. Consequently, a significant result of Composition's convergence is a clash between two dominant technologies that exist in the teaching of writing—computers and assessment—and the struggle between the two leaves many wondering which one (or if one) will fold into the other.

INTERTWINING TECHNOLOGIES: A SHORT HISTORY OF THE RISE OF COMPUTERS AND ASSESSMENT IN COMPOSITION

Computers and assessment not only represent competing technologies in contemporary Composition Studies; each also reflects a particular ideological domain in the teaching of writing. In these days of colleges and universities being driven by "fast capitalism," a mix of highly mobile capital and the rapid distribution of information plus capital through technological means (Kress, 1994), compositionists increasingly find themselves considering strange alliances in teaching writing to adapt to a new academic environment. For instance, some are developing various types of distance learning writing courses, integrating basic writing classes with "traditional" first-year composition, and linking writing to nonhumanities courses, to name but three critical changes in writing instruction. Yet few of these unions challenge a writing teacher's pedagogical philosophy in the same ways as online writing instruction and the questions of how to evaluate the work produced. This point is at the core of why computer-based composition remains at the periphery of writing instruction at many colleges and universities. When assessment drives instruction and there is no clear way to assess certain classroom activities, it becomes difficult for faculty members at some institutions to justify extensive use of materials that cannot be evaluated given the local infrastructure and values.

Just as the conventional psychometric understanding of writing assessment runs counter to many writing specialists' beliefs, for many compositionists so too does comprehending the place of computer-based composition in the teaching of writing. In either case, the technologies involved provide a resistance to both historical product–producer instructional methods and to measurement through accepted psychometric procedures. This makes it relatively easy for different factions within a writing program or an institution to dismiss the importance of teaching students through networked writing, because there is no recognized language available to writing teachers to explain the significance of having students write blogs, in MOOspace, or with hypertext, HTML, XML, and Perl script in terms of measuring student growth. Consequently, the underlying issue that exists for the current tension that technology raises for Composition is that very different ideas are at work for discussing students' knowledge making and knowledge producing in the writing process. We are still learning the language of how to describe and define what these knowledge making and knowledge producing processes are in the networked classroom space. Until such language becomes clearer for writing instructors, as Yancey (1999) outlined, creating a sense of coherence as to what we want from a student's electronic text or electronic portfolio is slippery at best.

However, some common points can link networked writing situations and writing assessment—the mystery is that writing specialists have not yet found where those commonalities lie. The Open Source Portfolio Initiative (OSPI) out of the University of Minnesota, for instance, proposes having an "industry standard" for electronic portfolios so that the look generates a sort of surface validity. Another commercialized system, LiveText, offers the generic rubric-based model for examining students' work from P-college. Unlike some of the other ideas offered later in this book, OSPI and LiveText simply import print-based criteria for rubrics to create a relational database or repository for student work. These options offer coherence in that the standards reflect a print-based understanding of what good writing is. Assessment then continues as it always has, except the material is uploaded into a program for safekeeping. This approach is fine if instructors continue having students write typical papers that are transformed into pixel and uploaded onto a site. However, such writing undervalues the incredible shift in literacy that the computer generated and how texts have responded. If instructors adopt portfolio programs like OSPI and LiveText, coherence does exist, but it is a surface coherence that may not necessarily fit together when reviewers closely examine the students' electronic texts.

At first glance, the dependence of one technological system on the other does seem quite remote, and the possibilities for coherence seem equally as remote, especially to the staunchest of practitioners in either the networked writing or assessment camp. To a great degree, networked writing and writing assessment do look like strange companions. Assessment talk often sounds retrograde, a reflection of an earlier era in writing instruction that prided itself on searching for an ideal text against which student writing was measured. Conversely, online writing instruction seems cutting-edge, a progressive examination of where Composition can travel if institutions have the faculty, the inclination, and the financial support to sustain the journey. The current situation in Composition reflects Guenther Kress' point that conventionality and change are often at odds (1995). Computers and writing assessment are at two ends of Composition's spectrum; each tells the tale of contemporary writing instruction—a cultural history rich in myths, memes, assumptions, promises, and speculations concerning what instructors can do with the available technologies and the transformations and results these technologies have on students' writing. Over the years, more than a few of these proposed ideas have bordered—if not crossed into—technomyopia, a condition futurist Paul Saffo (1992) described as the overestimation of the short-term potential of a new technology, and other ideas have been disproved of their value because of changing social, political, and economic conditions that affect writing instruction and evaluation and the widespread use of computers in teaching writing.

Guenther Kress saliently observed that although many think of technology as an "independently active agent in social affairs" (1999, p. 83), a message infused throughout society by the media and industry, any technology-dependent context—including writing classrooms—clearly requires particular social conditions for technologies to be adopted and to take hold in a culture. As a subset of literacy, writing is quite subject to changes in cultural or social conditions and can be thought of as a technological form, especially when it is compared with orality. Writing transformed Western culture's ways of making meaning, because it became the method of making meaning permanent. Similarly, assessment tools and Harvard's English A writing course were enacted to respond to specific social conditions in the late 1800s that demanded hierarchies exist in the workplace, in education, and in societal relations. Some device was needed to ensure a "professionalized" education to separate the managerial class from the aspiring working class. Thus, assessment mechanisms—a form of technology created to generate some meaning about student writing and to guarantee a measure of cultural reproduction—were put in place. For almost a century, this system worked well to make permanent certain notions about student writing because technological and social conditions stayed relatively stable. In the 1980s, with a third wave of technology entering American life through the computer chip, a dramatic shift occurred in the technological and social conditions connected to American writing instruction: Electronic or networked writing emerged. Kress, like Saffo, suggested that the shift from print literacy to visuality—with its remaking of linguistic rules, authorship, readership, publication, and scholarship—reflected a different set of cultural conditions that parallel the globalization, social distancing, and expansion of communication in American society (Kress, 1995, 1999; Saffo, 1992). Today, writing instructors realize that technology, assessment, and literacy are not separate from social conditions; rather, all are directly influenced by the swiftness of societal development and the pressures from varying social and political institutions.

Composition specialists need to be acutely aware of what we teach when we layer multiple technologies in the classroom, because Kress' observation reflects one of the potential common points in the convergence between networked writing and assessment: the pace of technological change. Generally, the rate of technological change in any culture, including Composition's, follows along a decades-long path before becoming fully accessible to all. Paul Saffo (1992) called this the "30-year rule." According to Saffo, the first decade generates excitement and bewilderment toward a technological product, but not many users. In the second decade, the technology creates societal flux, as standards ebb and flow to conform to the increased use of technology in mainstream culture. This second decade is the most chaotic, as the technological object undergoes a period that decides which forms or versions of the technology will succeed or fail in society. With the third decade comes a "so what?" response to the technology, because it has been fully assimilated, virtually ubiquitous, in society. By the 30-year mark, people are very familiar with the technology; some use it extensively, and others have moved on to new ideas or technologies.

If we apply Saffo's (1992) principles to the current technologies in the teaching of writing—computers and assessment—compositionists can see the following happening in Composition's culture:

1874—Harvard introduces written essay entrance exams (Berlin, 1987).

1885—Harvard begins Freshman Composition sequence (Berlin, 1987).

1890—Widespread inclusion of first-year composition as a university requirement in American colleges and universities. Shortly after came the first calls to abolish the freshman writing sequence (Connors, 1996).

1900s—Reemergence of graduate training in rhetoric (Connors, 1996).

1919—The College Board formed. First use of multiple-choice entrance exam for college admission.

1920—Expansion of undergraduate writing courses to include a sophomore-level writing class and advanced writing classes in composition, rhetoric, creative, and journalistic prose (Connors, 1996).

Mid-1920s—Carnegie Foundation begins psychometric evaluation for standard achievement using tens of thousands of Pennsylvania's high school and college students.

1920s—The efficiency model for teaching composition through Thorndike and Hillegas' quantitative evaluation scales is proposed and attempted. Similarly, current-traditional rhetorical practices begin to dominate college composition instruction (Berlin, 1987).

1926—The Scholastic Aptitude Test (SAT) first piloted.

1928—IBM starts working on a test-scoring machine with no success.

1930s—Composition instructors make the first call to focus on writing as a response to social contexts and to examine the writing process instead of the written product (Berlin, 1987).

1934—IBM purchases the Markograph system to improve its test-scoring machine.

1935—The Graduate Record Exam (GRE) begins.

1936—IBM's Markograph system scores Regents exams in New York and the Providence, Rhode Island, school district tests. Also, Harvard institutes an admissions policy that requires all students to take the SAT.

1937—The other Ivy League universities follow Harvard's lead and require the SAT for admission.

1939—The National Teacher Exam (NTE) begins (Lemann, 1995).

1939—Oscar James Campbell proposes abolishing first-year writing courses and replacing them with writing instruction infused in the students' subject matter. Campbell also charges that the first-year writing course structure constructs a system of devalued academic workers who are prevented from promotion. Campbell's argument is one of the first calls concerning writing across the curriculum and the teaching conditions for compositionists (Berlin, 1987).

Mid-1940s—Rise of the general education component to accommodate the influx of students who took advantage of the G.I. Bill after World War II (Lemann, 1995).

1948—Educational Testing Service (ETS) emerges.

1957—Federal funds first invested in the teaching of composition and literature in American colleges and universities (Berlin, 1987).

1958—American College Testing (ACT) begins (Berlin, 1987; Lemann, 1995).

1960s—Large amount of rhetoric instruction begins at the undergraduate level (Berlin, 1987).

1961—Paul Diederich develops the analytical scale for evaluating student writing (Berlin, 1987).

1966—Ellis Page and Dieter Paulus, among others, study intrinsic elements of writing, such as punctuation and parts of speech, to analyze and approximately measure student writing with computer technology. A shorthand form for the algorithm becomes *trins* (intrinsic attributes) and *proxes* (approximate measures; Lemann, 1995).

1966—Project Essay Grade (PEG) created to become a cost-effective alternative to human essay graders. PEG is based on an algorithm that reads trins and proxes (Lemann, 1995).

1972—Harold Slotnick develops a computer essay grading system derived from the factor analysis of six different trins correlated with specific proxes. These statistical findings were to provide a better understanding of what characteristics student writing maintained to elicit certain judgments made by either a human or a computerized reader (Huot, 1996).

1977—Frequency word count system (the Standard Frequency Index) is constructed to analyze the words used by two different student writers when composing on the same theme (Huot, 1996).

1977—The Primary-Trait Scoring Model emerges (Faigley, Cherry, Jolliffe, & Skinner, 1985). A shift occurs from norm-referenced assessment to criterion-referenced assessment in writing instruction.

Early 1980s—Rise of the portfolio as a form of direct, authentic writing assessment (Belanoff & Dickson, 1991).

1984—Steve Jobs introduces the Macintosh computer to make the world of computing easier and more enjoyable. Macintosh computers become the preferred computer to teach writing because of their simplicity.

1985—Lester Faigley and others call for performative writing assessment to evaluate student writers' knowledge and their composing processes (Faigley et al., 1985).

Mid to late 1980s—Rise of social constructivism in Composition and the beginning of electronic communities via e-mail.

1992—Emil Roy produces a prototype computerized student placement model, the Structured Decision System (SDS), which maintains face and construct validity but falls short with concurrent and predictive validity (Lemann, 1995).

1995—Ellis Page and Nancy Peterson update the 1966 PEG system to conform to contemporary computer hardware and software (Lemann, 1995).

1997—Announcement of a "new" essay grading software program developed by psychology professors with an interest in psycholinguistics. The Intelligent Essay Assessor is a joint venture between the University of Colorado and New Mexico State University.

1997—Forefronting of electronic portfolios as the primary assessment tool for networked writing instruction (Huot, 1998).

1999—ETS begins total computer-generated essay scoring of the GMAT (ETS, 1999). ETS intends to phase in complete computer essay scoring for all writing components over a 5-year period.

1999—Kathleen Blake Yancey suggests a "fourth wave" ahead for writing assessment to address textual changes caused by computer-assisted writing instruction (Yancey, 1999).

The reason for working through this timeline is not only to see the complexity of Composition's cultural history related to computers and writing assessment but also to note how the 30-year rule sets up a type of spiraling path of development for each through the teaching of writing. As writing assessment moves through Composition, so does computer technology.

It is interesting to note how these two technologies intersect and counter each other at various points in time. For example, just as written entrance essay exams became a familiar item in the admissions process, in 1919, the multiple-choice exam emerged. This movement reflected a change in education's social conditions. Learning had entered a period that had educators elevating a scientific or behaviorist model as the way for measuring student achievement. The behaviorist model of learning ushered in the notion that writing, like other learning activities, could be machine scored efficiently and effectively.

In Composition, the spiraling development of computer technology and writing assessment appeared to take an almost clear 30-year path. In 1936, IBM established itself in the grading of essays using the Markograph system. In 1966 a computerized parsing system based on trins and proxes was created to measure discrete word items in students' writing. Through various refinements in trins and proxes word counts, by 1995, an essay grading software program emerged. This idea was further expanded on until 1997 with software packages like the Intelligent Essay Assessor (still patent pending), CyberQ, the commercialized Vantage system (now defunct), and ETS's WritePlacer (now AccuPlacer), which emerged to handle placement exams. Now, in mid-2004, Pearson Education has offered The College Board use of its version of essay-grading software to handle the 2005 SAT Essay Writing component. In essence, what has happened to Composition's culture, just as what happens in most cultures that rely on technology, is the idea of coevolution between computers and writing assessment, that is, a series of changes in technological means that respond to the "complex interplay of perceived needs, competitive and political pressures, and social and [other] technological innovations" (Fidler, 1997, p. 23).

Many of these perceived needs, competitive and political pressures, and social or other innovations come from outside the field of Composition. In the 1920s, only a couple of decades after Harvard instituted its Freshman A model, compositionists could see the external pressures begin. In 1919, The College Board opened. Shortly thereafter, ETS started its operation followed by ACT. The entrenchment of multiple-choice, or indirect, writing assessment became apparent in the 1950s. As James A. Berlin (1987) observed, during the same period, the rise of undergraduate instruction in multiple rhetorics occurred between 1940 and 1960. It appears that rather than having writing assessment drive instruction at the college level, writing specialists of that era established a countermeasure to the then-current psychometric technology in place.

Again, in the 1970s, when essay-grading software systems took root as the first phase of convergence in writing assessment, another countermeasure also began to rise. In the early 1980s, Pat Belanoff, Peter Elbow, and Lester Faigley among others pushed for more direct, performative forms for evaluating student writing. By the early 1980s, teaching college writing in response to multiple rhetorics was commonplace, and indirect writing assessment needed to give way to researchers' discoveries that evaluation needed to match what students were learning in the classroom. As a result, portfolios appeared as the answer for engaging in performative student writing assessment. Essay-grading software became overshadowed by Composition's embracing of the portfolio. However, essay-grading software did not fall far from view over the last 30 years even though compositionists were not necessarily paying attention until the developers made some bold announcements about the Intelligent Essay Assessor and the program's ability to grade essays more efficiently and effectively than teachers could.

As Composition begins the 21st century, many writing teachers have reached a "so what?" stage regarding writing assessment practices, as their familiarity with the portfolio has taken hold. This searching is particularly true if instructors are heavily invested in computer literacy and they need to discover ways to blend current trends in writing assessment with networked writing activities. We appear to be in the second phase of convergence between the two technologies as Saffo's 30 year progression seems to show another intersecting point. This time the struggle seems to be whether essay-grading software will overtake the portfolio. If so, what will writing instruction and assessment look like in the future for all levels, K through 20?

This is not a silly question to ask. Since 1997, with the most recent fusing of writing assessment and computer technologies, Composition finds itself at the point of convergence, that is, a place where "diverse technologies and forms of media are coming together" (Fidler, 1997, p. 23) to evolve into a single way to communicate. Through the processes of coevolution and convergence, technologies eventually find ways to coexist and mutually influence all systems.

In convergence, a gradual metamorphosis occurs and blends the important qualities of one technological form with competing technologies. Over time, the technologies involved either adapt or propagate into new forms. If the technologies in question do not adapt, generally they wither and die.

Because it appears as though networked writing and writing assessment are at a critical point in their mutual development, compositionists must watch how the two technologies adapt in the near future. If current writing assessment practices do not adapt more quickly to networked environments, it stands to reason that these practices and discourse will most likely cease to exist as a legitimate form to discuss student work. Similarly, if networked writing instruction does not accommodate some recognized form of assessment, it too will fade from Composition's culture because of a lack of institutional and financial support.

Given the current social, political, and economic conditions surrounding higher education (and K–12 education as well), few institutions will support or adopt one of these technologies—or a blending of the two—without just cause. This is why Composition appears to be headed for some important choices in the convergence process. The steps taken in the next few years in networked writing instruction and in writing assessment, in all likelihood, will affect Composition's value as a program of study inside the academy.

Recently, Cynthia Selfe and Kathleen Blake Yancey, respectively, put forward the possible transformations in computer-mediated writing instruction and assessment practices (Selfe, 1999; Yancey, 1999). In separate articles published concurrently, these two scholars recognized the influence of technology on various literacy practices and the awareness that compositionists must develop to move ahead in our pedagogical practices. Taken together, Selfe's and Yancey's articles suggest that Composition has begun to acknowledge the convergence that has been creeping up on the field over the last several years. Only now, as we are in the middle of a second round of convergence, can researchers provide us with the language for what has been permeating our culture. Yancey (1999) recognized that the cross-impact of technological convergence via the computer is one aspect of writing assessment's "fourth wave" (p. 500), in which noncanonical, hybrid texts like e-mail, hypertext, MOOs, blogs, or other web-based works challenge established methods of evaluation.

Yancey is correct in her observations. These newer electronic texts do challenge traditionally established methods of evaluation. However, writing program administrators and faculty need to be aware that from the point of recognizing convergence, a workable assessment project for networked writing will most likely require an entire generation (a period of 20–30 years) before wide-scale adoption occurs and habituated practices related to the fourth wave of writing assessment take hold. For many of us who are teaching now, that time frame nearly represents our entire academic life.

Still, this does not mean that those of us currently teaching in networked classrooms or evaluating electronic texts under various assessment models cannot put forward new directions for some future hybrid form of networked writing and assessment. We should. Actually, we need to provide models that try, fail, and succeed in some areas as convergence unfolds. There are too many outside of Composition who will put forward trends in both networked writing and writing assessment that run counter to the pedagogical principles inherent in each aspect of writing instruction. Our history shows this to be true in the past. Our literature shows this to be true in the present. Writing teachers have the ability to enact changes in the classroom that affect the future, and this ability includes discovering effective ways for blending networked writing and assessment.

For most of the last decade while the two technologies have been simultaneously evolving, many in the forefront of both writing assessment and networked writing instruction have displayed technomyopia. In the field's literature, the leading proponents for each side have overestimated the classroom potential for their respective forms of technology and have chided the opposition when the other side's technology falls short of expectations. The language of "promise and paradox" (Selfe, 1997) echoes in much of Composition's literature on computers and writing. The promise and paradox discourse reflects the puzzlement and excitement writing teachers felt in the early stages of computers and writing instruction. Anecdotal evidence worked well to introduce writing programs and their faculties to the potential for computers in the writing classroom. Now, though, a fair number of colleges and universities have some form of computer labs, "smart" classrooms, and distance learning facilities available for their teachers and students. Composition as a field is well into the second, almost third, decade of computers in the classroom. The language of promise and paradox should not be as dominant as it still seems to be.

Assessment, although it maintains a slightly longer history in Composition than computers do, also displays a healthy dose of the language of promise and paradox. The promise is that each new wave of assessment practices will tell instructors and administrators more about their students and the students' achievement in writing; the paradox is that high schools, colleges, and universities seem to test more, ask for more learning outcomes, and know less about their students' writing abilities.

We can also see this language of promise and paradox in relation to convergence through Composition's general condemnation of essay-grading software and widespread celebration of electronic portfolios as the way to measure students' online writing. Although electronic portfolios do reflect the current common ground for computer and assessment technologies, by no means should portfolios—even electronic ones—remain a fixed constant in a dynamic system. Other writing assessment procedures must be looked at as well, including older methods of evaluating writing, to see what has been valued in the past (and whether instructors still value those characteristics) and whether those methods can be updated to fit current literacy expectations. For instance, although electronic holistic essay scoring may seem regressive for all the same reasons analogous to traditional essay scoring, some may view the process as a first step toward developing a writing assessment tool that is more ecologically balanced for the networked classroom in certain institutions. The issue at hand is that instructors cannot stay complacent with any current blended assessment method, regardless of how it compares with present habituated pedagogical practices.

Without composition specialists working on the revision and refinement of these converged tools, our current methods may stay static for far longer than their usefulness. Although the efficiency rates of a software program like the Intelligent Essay Assessor or Pearson's ECS may sound impressive today to cost-conscious administrators, computer-savvy compositionists must present alternative assessment plans that reflect greater accuracy, consistency, and performative value for classroom use. Like hundreds of other types of writing tools made for the computer, a particular evaluation software program's value may be limited in scope or in its purpose. If such software systems are adopted at a high cost to the institution, many writing programs and instructors will be stuck with a potential assessment albatross. That is why it is becoming increasingly more important for compositionists working on alternative assessment concepts to work alongside networked writing to push for different, visible evaluation strategies in the years ahead.

From my perspective, there seem to be five points that teaching faculty and composition scholars should concern themselves with as networked writing and assessment evolve into the same environments: (a) the relative advantages of this hybrid over other, earlier existing forms of computer-based writing and writing assessment; (b) the compatibility this hybridized form will have with more established models and pedagogies; (c) the level of technological complexity and sophistication needed to implement the hybrid in a typical college classroom; (d) the reliability and validity of the hybrid in networked classroom settings; and (e) the ability to observe and repeat similar writing and assessment practices in networked classrooms found at different educational levels (2-year colleges, 4-year liberal arts schools, comprehensive universities, research universities, etc.). As writing programs search locally for new ideas to handle these whirlwind days of providing writing assessment and networked writing in the same classroom space, these two competing technologies will continue to converge. Ignoring technological convergence does not make its advancement go away, nor does belittling writing assessment in our networked writing classes reduce the possibility of it happening. On the contrary, dismissing either idea only makes writing programs' catch-up plans so much more difficult and more susceptible to the decisions of others.

So here is where my argument begins. In some ways, mine is a simple argument. New technological times are ushering in a second phase of convergence for Composition, particularly in the ways that writing teachers evaluate their students' work. Although this seems to be a basic statement to many involved in the teaching of writing, the problems that arise when educators try to enact so much as a minute change in the classroom dynamic—such as constructing a workable computer lab configuration for writing classes or deciding to purchase wireless laptop computers versus desktop computers for a student lab—become highly complex. When writing teachers or their program administrators attempt to merge two very involved technologies like networked writing and writing assessment, we frequently expect something that looks like Composition's Gordian knot to occur.

But the knot must be cut. If not by compositionists, then others surely will do the cutting. If writing programs do not attend to their own assessment and networked writing needs in tandem, others will speak, legislate, or mandate for them. This is not an idle threat to our work. Anyone who follows *The Chronicle of Higher Education* understands that the advance in computer-based essay grading is a frequent topic for the newspapers' technology beat writers. Although many compositionists cry foul and deride the fixed definitions of literacy put forward by these efforts and reports, people outside Composition recognize the significance of technological convergence on writing assessment. The general public seems to find this topic newsworthy as well. *Salon* and *USA Today* have published several stories about writing instruction, electronic essay grading, and writing assessment over the last few years. By controlling the means of presenting stories about technology in both networked writing and writing assessment, reporters and the media also control the language used to discuss these topics—especially for the general public. If Composition loses control over its own language, its subaltern status in the academy is almost guaranteed to remain well into the 21st century.

This book, then, attempts to examine the ramifications of convergence in Composition with the aim of describing just how extensive the transformation may be for the habitual practices and common beliefs teachers have for evaluating students' written work. It is my hope to do more in this book than praise one side's efforts while damning another. These types of arguments are not productive for finding new avenues to change our writing assessment practices in an age of networked instruction. Rather than think of networked writing and writing assessment as two separate entities within Composition, as many tend to do, I want to examine the context as an intertwining spiral that lives in each of our classroom spaces.

Because these two technologies are changing the nature of writing instruction and evaluation, so too must instructors' thinking and language change to envision and discuss what lies ahead without relying on technomyopia or technophobia. Convergence requires more than a set of new metaphors to classify the information at hand; it depends on a new framework for understanding how people compose and interact through networked discourse and how college writing departments and programs can evaluate these new written forms that arise from digital literacy. Convergence demands compositionists to rethink what we value about our long history with technology, about written texts, about the use of technology in the classroom, and about the place of assessment in our daily teaching.

And so, this is where my discussion begins.

Chapter 1

Moving Toward Internetworked Writing and Assessment

Words and the texts they produce are the bonds of Internet culture, just as they are the bonds of Composition's culture. David Porter, writing in *Internet Culture*, best summarized the prominence of language that exists within networked spaces: "Whatever else Internet culture might be, it is still largely a text-based affair. Words are not simply tools which we can use in any way we see fit. They come to us framed by specific histories of use and meaning, and are products of particular ideological struggles" (1996, p. 6). We could substitute the word *composition* for *Internet* and the intended meaning continues to hold. Both worlds are indeed text-based affairs, regardless of whatever else they might be. Yet, students who write in online environments display a marked difference compared with those students writing in a real classroom setting, as many writing instructors can attest. There is something transformative about teaching writing in networked space. The computer, a maze of wires and circuits in a box, recasts the writing process into something alive and genuine for students. Instructors who teach Composition in networked environments have suggested this point for years, both in lore and in the literature.

But, what is this "something" that marks the difference between virtual and real classroom spaces? How do we name this "something," and more important, what do we value about this "something" that happens in the writing classroom when we move from print to pixel? From what I observe in my own classes as students post to their discussion lists, enter MOOs and adopt new identities through making textual choices, develop weblogs for themselves and for classes, and construct web pages for friends, clients, or organizations, it seems that the computer quite clearly converts the process of writing into the process of communication. In turn, students see how words carry certain historical contexts of use and meaning as well as how words can retain particular ideological references that reflect larger struggles.

Unfortunately, often writing and communication are two separate processes in composition courses. Perhaps this division arises from Composition's connections to *belles lettres* and English departments, in which students write to express their feelings and little else. In these situations, writing does not necessarily have to be produced for a reader's understanding. Many times, especially in first-year composition, writing can be a private exercise. And it is true that for most of us, writing is a private exercise. One only has to look at the personal notes he or she takes at a meeting or in a lecture, or at the journal entries written for a class or personal expression, or at certain affected academic or fictive styles in scholarship and literature that are studied in the classroom to realize that writing is not always meant to be understood. However, when writing communicates, ideas must be presented to others and acted upon by granting a response. Writing as communication demands public acknowledgment. Without a response, there is no communication. If there is no communication happening, then there is no understanding as to whether one's words make meaning or fall silent. Consequently, the act of communicating depends on writers targeting those ideas, elements, and languages that frequently run counter to academic prose.

Online writing makes for a perfect example of writing as a communicative act, because it entails that a reply should come from others. Some forms of online writing, like blogs, MOOs, or e-mails, demand replies from others. Without a return acknowledgment of some sort, a posting carries little meaning for a community. As a communicative act, then, online writing makes material Paulo Freire's observation:

> Only through communication can human life hold meaning. The teacher's thinking is authenticated only by the authenticity of the students' thinking. The teacher cannot think for his students nor can he impose his thought on them. Authentic thinking, thinking that is concerned about *reality*, does not take place in ivory tower isolation, but only in communication. (1993, p. 58)

It is the "public" characteristic of online writing that infuses the words with meaning and elevates them to a communicative act. To write publicly means that student writers make their words available to all in the course or in cyberspace, not just for the exclusive private classroom relationship built on paper between student writer and instructor or the semi-public partnership peer groups evoke. Following Freire, then, in genuine public discourse settings, such as those found online, the instructor is not the sole authenticator for student thought as he or she most likely is in private classroom contexts. The instructor's voice is just one of many voices responding to the words. The polysemic quality and the concept of transforming the classroom writing experience into a real, communicative, public activity are two critical aspects of what writing instructors value about online writing.

This real, communicative, public function of student writing in internetworked spaces revolutionizes Composition and holds out promises for practitioners that writing will be removed from the skill-and-drill and current–traditional approaches to writing instruction. Yet this same liberatory quality can confound the use of traditional writing assessment models to evaluate student growth and development in the writing classroom. This latter point becomes a thorny issue for K–20 writing teachers, as federal and state legislative demands for accountability push us to ensure that certain basic writing standards are being met in the classroom. As many English education specialists, education theorists, composition researchers, and K–12 teachers will suggest, these political expectations for leaving no child behind frequently reconstruct writing classroom settings that return teaching to the spoon feeding of information so students can pass minimally challenging state writing exams (Apple, 2001, 2003; Hillocks, 2002).

Computer-assisted writing pedagogy offers the potential to break students' "banking concept of education" (1993, p. 53) so familiar in Freire's readings and so commonly found in a majority of writing assessment systems. In public, networked spaces, students learn that others beyond the teacher's voice can authenticate their words and imbue the students' words with meaning. For experienced or comfortable writers, this can be a liberating moment in the classroom. However, for students at ease with the banking concept of education in the writing classroom, the freedom can be unnerving—if not downright confusing. After all, if students are saturated with a top-down educational model that focuses mostly on grades, test scores, and teacher perceptions, then any classroom writing activities that move beyond this paradigm will be met with students' attitudinal resistance or cognitive dissonance. All too often, these reactions are discovered in instructors' student evaluations at the end of the term. A recent anonymous response written in a course evaluation from one of my College Composition II classes indicates the potential problem for some students who find public writing and the abandonment of the banking concept of education discomforting:

> Some would say they [our writing classes] are not as productive as I thought [they were] because they [other students] are used to, and find comfort in, a traditional (boring) classroom. I'm sure sometimes classes went against Dr. Penrod's lesson planbook [sic], but I found every one productive (fall 1998 semester, brackets mine for clarity).

This student aptly points to the difficulties some of his or her peers may have with a writing classroom that responds to technological convergence. The current–traditional or purely process-based composition class, or a writing class focused solely on meeting expectations for state writing assessment exams, read as a "boring" writing classroom by this student, has set opportunities for the students' composing processes. Productivity in the traditional writing classroom is defined by many students, professors, and programs as how many words or pages are churned out, how efficient those words or pages are in relation to a real or perceived template for good writing, and how those words or pages are legitimated by an instructor's grade. Composition's convergence with technology transforms this older notion of productivity. In this particular composition class that I taught, "productivity" became redefined as students interacted with their ideas through the use of computers and different media forms (both print and electronic) as they wrote about their views for and with others. Instead of students imitating a model for good writing, the students' online interactions were used to establish benchmarks for what good writing was within the contexts of different course assignments.

I found it telling that in the evaluation, this student mentioned my having a lesson plan book to guide my daily actions in the classroom. (I do not use one. I do have a syllabus, but points of flexibility are built into the course design to accommodate an extra day of discussion, research, or writing whenever needed.) The student's comments reflect the reality that, whether personally or institutionally imposed, many writing teachers do adhere to a strict sequence when teaching composition and that any disruption in the order fouls up the semester's learning activities. This student's observation underscores how "learning productivity" is often defined in education, as following an inflexible schedule of events that culminates in a capstone assignment or course.

Here, too, computer-based writing instruction alters the method of delivering course content, which shifts our understanding of "productivity." As writing instructors have found, in an interactive, networked environment, it is difficult to keep a rigid lesson plan or course schedule. This is because the faculty member frequently responds to multiple, individualized situations in the students' writing and thinking processes. Depending on the students' comfort levels with technology, some can move forward quickly whereas others take much more time to accomplish the same task. Usually, in computer-based classroom environments, I have found that the simpler the syllabus structure, the easier it is to maintain a sense of direction and a sense of discovery for both instructors and students. That way, students can move at their own paces, and I can tweak instruction to serve where the students are in the course. This seems to me to be more productive learning, although the course looks and feels chaotic at times.

The concept of productivity must be redefined when computer technology is introduced into the writing classroom. Whether using electronic discussion lists, web writing, hypertexts, MOOs, and the like, the classroom always centers on the word and the ability of others besides the instructor to discern meaning (not to mention increasing the students' potential for developing solid grammatical and spelling skills so a computer can respond to their commands). Productivity no longer refers to a set number of words or pages to be churned out; rather, productivity connects to how effectively writers communicate in a given context. All this alleviates the need for an instructor to follow a rigid daily or weekly structure, because he or she constantly surrounds the students with writing practice. The computer's potential for releasing instructors from the confines of their planning books allows them to reach the roots of what writing instruction needs to be and what student writers need to learn—how to control their thoughts and language to communicate with an audience, regardless of genre. Students then begin to discover for themselves the power of the written word, as real audiences respond to their ideas while a machine carries out their requests.

This pedagogical change is not unrecognized by students, who frequently react to the instructional shift in a positive manner. Instead of instructors telling students how to write, or explaining to students which models to use in their writing, or even demonstrating to students what to put on the blank screen in front of them, computer-based composition classes inspire students to take responsibility for their education. As a result, students' enthusiasm and interest toward the course increase. This point was made clearer to me after a student in a College Composition II class wrote in his or her final evaluation: "We continue discussions about topics and work outside of class by use of classlists (e-mail)" and "By using hands-on techniques and modern technology, she [the professor] conveys the ideas of College Comp II in a way that the youth of today can understand" (fall, 1998).

Students who come to our writing classes with little experience in technology—albeit this type of student is becoming increasingly rarer but still does exist in some places—can benefit from these experiences. Several students wrote in their student evaluations that although they were nervous entering a course that had such a heavy focus on technology and writing, "the lectures and assignments were interesting" and "the information learned will help me in the future" (fall, 2003). Infusing technology into the writing process made quite a few students think of themselves as "professional writers" because they had "the opportunity to discover and present their work in a professional forum on line" (fall 2003). This dimension of having students see themselves as writers with a real audience is important for them to take genuine ownership of their work.

The computer's promise is great for enacting Freire's (1993) "authentic reflection" in undergraduate students' writing processes. Using online contexts, students develop a consciousness about their writing simultaneously with learning about the world around them. They begin to see that without another's recognition of their words, writing has no purpose. In essence, electronic communication offers students a chance to see themselves as writers with an audience. Once student writers are aware of themselves as being real writers with something to say, they acknowledge—as this student did—that their writing courses "open up the realm of greater research or more effort, time, and overall work being put into a single paper or project" (fall, 1998). This is an important step for undergraduates to accept in the writing process, especially in the latter sequences of first-year composition devoted to argument, research writing, and audience reaction.

As Freire suggested, students who reflect on themselves and on the world in communication with others "increase the scope of their perception" and "begin to direct their observations towards previously inconspicuous phenomena" (1993, p. 63). Again, let me draw on another comment from a final course evaluation to illustrate the effect that technological convergence has for encouraging students to develop the type of self-awareness about their writing that composition faculty aim for each semester Regarding how students have come to recognize elements in their writing over the term, in the evaluation this particular student says that the blend of networked activities in the class "emphasized the difference between informal writing and argumentative writing. I felt comfortable writing informally before I took this course. Now I also feel comfortable writing argumentatively" (fall, 1998). For this student, just as for others like him or her, the mix of writing and thinking in different media and in different genres not only helped this person recognize discursive changes but also aided the student in developing a comfort zone when writing with different levels of formality.

What is it about computer-based writing environments that elicits these types of student remarks, none of which are uncommon, as we read in journal articles and hear in conference papers by our colleagues who also practice computer-assisted writing instruction? As mentioned earlier in this chapter, online writing activities accentuate the private–public split in the composing process. However, technology inverts what we think is private and public. Although each of us may have private thoughts, once those thoughts are typed into a networked space like e-mail or the web, our minds link with other minds. So, the mind's private actions are made public instead of being kept unstated. This is especially true with certain electronic genres like weblogs, as the online journal format promotes the mind's continual reflection and private action. The body, which is public in most social spaces, becomes private when we communicate electronically. Unless all of us share the same physical classroom space at some point in the semester, the students and the instructor may not know what others look like in the class or from where the students respond. When we compose asynchronously, we do not know how the writer looks. Most likely, we do not want to know this information. We certainly do not know who our audience is or what the members look like when we correspond with others on discussion lists or at gaming sites.

However, instructors know that when students are sending us e-mail in the wee hours, they are writing and thinking long after the day's class is over. When students send their instructors postings about something that occurs related to a class that was taken a year or two ago (or more) and resonated with the student's experience in the class, then teachers know that writing, thinking, and reflecting remain part of that student's learning process.

NEW MEDIA/NEW RISKS FOR WRITERS AND THEIR INSTRUCTORS

As mentioned in the last section, instead of the corporeal aspects of writing in the classroom (the physical acts of letter formation or putting pen to paper, for instance), the mental features of communicating with others becomes highlighted when we shift to computers. For certain student populations in our writing classes, the celebration of the mental process over the body in composing is an important shift. As Leigh Kobert, one of my graduate students who also worked in the medical publishing field, pointed out in a post to our class list in Writing for Electronic Communities, a graduate writing class I teach, in the spring 1999 semester,

> One of the early readings described "disembodied voices and decontextualized points of view." However, I can think of a context in which this disconnection is very welcome. As I believe I have said I work with people with physical and learning disabilities. Some of the people I talk to struggle just to get out a sentence. Rheingold touches on the factor of people with disabilities, i.e., CMC [Computer Mediated Communication] allows the to be treated as they have always wanted to be "as thinkers and transmitters of ideas and feeling beings." It must be incredibly freeing to experience a medium for once without the disability being the first thing that everyone is aware of. There is at last a chance to be judged outside the vessel of a limited body or speech/hearing disabilities.

Leigh described an appealing situation for many reticent students, especially for those with medical or physical conditions that hamper face-to-face (F2F) communication. The celebration of the mind over the body in computer-based writing allows greater numbers of students to participate because of technological innovations that make communication possible for students with disabilties. However, faceless interactivity is also a rhetorical context full of risks for a writer. Howard Rheingold (1991) observed that some online writers are hampered by the disconnectedness and decontextualization that can occur with electronic communication. That seems to be true; gregarious students, who enjoy a live audience for their ideas, frequently have difficulties making the move to computer-based writing activities. And there are still many students who value being present in a traditional classroom interacting with instructors and peers. Of course, it is also important to mention the digital divide that separates families with computers from those without (or families with broadband vs. those who have dial-up access). For varying reasons, all these students find themselves feeling vulnerable or disadvantaged in computer-based writing classes because of the disconnectedness and decontextualization that can occur with asynchronous writing.

A second, but equally important, risk in online communication is a "panoptical" effect that occurs with some participants. Periodically, the experience of writing for discussion lists or for web sites is compared to Foucault's description of Jeremy Bentham's Panopticon, where everyone is seen or read, so each person monitors accordingly his or her thoughts and language. To clarify this for the classroom experience, a panoptical effect describes a situation in which students' posted words and ideas are observed by everyone participating during that writing session. As I said earlier, networked writing is almost always public, even in classroom settings. In fact, the only private form of networked writing that might exist is when a writer posts a message to him or herself as a reminder or to archive later. Otherwise, online conversations are meant for public view and reaction. Some students respond to this circumstance by self-censoring or self-monitoring their replies to the group. Others react to the constant sending and receiving of messages by tapping into the relationships formed on screen (some of which may or may not seep into F2F class encounters) or by constructing a different personality from the one presented in the classroom. This latter option is done when students wish to avoid the panoptical effect and speak freely. Their construction of a new identity masks their real presence in virtual space.

If this comparison of networked writing to the Panopticon is an accurate one, then writing in linked classroom spaces continually requires student writers to contemplate their audience beyond the private exchanges with a professor or classmate or the semipublic interaction with a peer group. Some students may find that constant observation of their words in computer-mediated writing environments forces them to always watch their words or risk the ire of their classmates or others in on the discussion. When interacting with ideas in electronic environments, however, writers frequently find they cannot watch what they say as they might do in a F2F class. Should a discourse rule be broken, the violator will soon learn that classmates will watch his or her words for the writer.

Students in my fall 2003 writing classes connected to online environments proposed a new risk—the problem of trust. Theorists like Howard Rheingold (2003) suggest that as students become more savvy regarding electronically mediated communication, it is harder for them to trust who is writing on the other end of the post. The students cited numerous violations of trust in written communication found in online conversations as promoting the Panoptical effect, from police posing as teenagers to sting pedophiles to kids posing as psychics in a chat room; the ability for others to pose as someone they are not puts many students in a state of unease. Even for many who write responses online for class discussions, their concerns as to who might be on the other side of the screen is enough for them to watch what they say. This may be particularly true for international students, who are quite concerned about the U.S. Patriot Act and how it could play out for them in academic settings. Consequently, writing teachers need to discuss student concerns related to trust, because it is a vital part of the communication process. As Francis Fukuyama noted, "trust does not reside in integrated circuits or fiber optic cables" (1995, p. 25). A sense of community frequently can and does reside in integrated circuits, however, and if we hope to establish writing communities in networked environments, particularly in educational settings, trust building needs to be part of the ongoing discussions related to writing.

A third risk is the student's use of silence in an online environment. In traditional classroom spaces, frequently an instructor can tell whether a student's silence means assent, dissent, disinterest, skepticism, thoughtfulness, or withdrawal by watching the student's body language and reactions to the events surrounding him or her. This is not the case with online writing instruction. Silent students—the lurkers—may be put at a disadvantage in cyberspace because their quietude could be misinterpreted as lack of interest. Writing teachers must also consider a student's silence as being a sign of mistrust of the online writing situation or of some other communication breach just as it might be inexperience with technology.

Because asynchronous writing assignments do not have students in direct physical contact with instructors, it is important to consider students' online silence as maintaining some substance. As sociolinguist Adam Jaworski noted, silence does suggest that some type of activity occurs (1993, p. 81). There may exist a formulaic element to a student's use of silence in online discussions. For instance, a student may remain silent because she has nothing of relevance to add to the discussion at a particular point. Or a student could be silent because his reading of the posts suggest that only old information is being repeated, and he feels there is nothing more to say about the topic. Jaworski (1993) also posited that there are some silences, such as pauses, which mark an individual's underlying personality characteristics and reflect that person's speech patterns. Thus, instructors cannot necessarily jump to conclusions with lurkers on a class list, because their silence may be far more substantive than frequent posters to the list.

Even chancier than the risks some students take in their responses is how a writing instructor evaluates an ongoing online discussion. On the one hand, students are writing—generally producing volumes of fluid and fluent text. They are using voice, tone, rhetorical strategies and appeals, and all the techniques and identity markers that professors expect of students when writing exposition or persuasion. And students are doing this without having the instructor tell the class how to use these tools.

However, the context in which students prepare the writing is extremely different from classroom assignments, journal writing, or most types of writing that teachers have come to expect. The students' writing is immediate and not filtered, as it might be in a F2F classroom, a journal entry, or a class assignment. Sometimes the mechanics, grammar, and spelling are a bit rough. Yet in a composition course influenced by technological convergence, I would argue that these students are often quite literate, especially if they are highly engaged in the topic under discussion. So, how does one evaluate such work? Numeric grades and letter equivalents seem inadequate to address the attentiveness, observations, and connections students make in their online discussions. Equally insufficient is the offering of "checks and minuses" for their participation, because the richness of the exchanges often points out the inadequacy of what a check or minus can tell us about a student's work. Moreover, grading solely on the surface mechanics of student postings seems thoroughly bogus to me because students are communicating with each other at a deeper level. In so many instances, students are correctly using the rhetorical concepts or techniques presented in class; it is just that their minds and fingers are moving so quickly that error occurs. We know from earlier composition research that when a student's mind is engaged at deeper levels or he or she is struggling with ideas, the writer's grammar suffers until the thoughts are sufficiently worked through.

Still, not assigning some type of value to students' online work is also inadequate, especially if I find myself teaching a class where all assignments are connected to internetworked activities. My ambivalence toward being responsive to my students' emergent ability as technorhetors and being responsible to my institution's demands on me as a professor mirrors Michael Day's "grading hand" observation (2000). Sometimes instructors' comments and grades interfere too regularly in the students' writing process, much to the detriment of the students' progress. Yet some type of evaluation needs to be in place to show accountability to my department, college, and university administration. Writing teachers in networked environments constantly need to be attentive to how much intervention is needed—if any at all—to evaluate the written work produced on a discussion list, a web site, a MOO, and so on. Day may be correct when he says faculty members might be better to leave e-mail exchanges ungraded, much like the way journals and journal writing functioned in earlier years (2000, p. 161). But what does that suggest for the other forms of networked writing students do in their classes?

Although Day's approach for leaving e-mail ungraded works for now, I wonder whether it will still be a viable option in forthcoming years, especially as students come to college more computer-savvy and fluent in writing for online audiences. These students will expect some type of grading on discussion list work because they have been steeped in an educational and a political system that demands writing be assessed, and the check and minus system may not carry sufficient value in the future. As for assessing web pages, MOO work, hypertext, and so on, compositionists have not truly addressed this issue in great depth other than to consider electronic portfolios. Assessment in these areas is still nascent, and greater thought needs to be given to how composition faculties are to evaluate this new form of writing. Rubrics alone will not be enough to handle the complexities and the variables that arise when one writes in electronic genres.

For the last 5 years, I have thought about the problems of assessing computer-generated writing assignments. Shirley Brice Heath's essay, "The Fourth Vision: Literate Language at Work," keeps coming to my mind as a way to outline broadly the type of identity-building and literacy experiences students have when writing in networked spaces and how instructors might evaluate those experiences. Heath's remarks offer the best defense for writing teachers to argue against using their grading hand too early in the development of their students' electronic writing experiences. For Heath,

> Being literate means being able to talk with and listen with others to interpret texts, say what they mean, link them to personal experience with other texts, argue with them and make predictions from them. develop future scenarios, compare and evaluate related situations, and know that practice of all these literate abilities is practical. (1990, p. 298)

Reflecting on my own experiences with students first coming to internetworked writing, I could see firsthand what Heath described about literate language, but it appears that there is no way, no language outside of the grading hand, to assess students' writing when it resists conforming to the traditional models. Technology-enhanced writing assignments undermine the instructor's power to legitimate a student's work because of the communicative freedom that discussion lists, web sites, MOOs, hypertexts, and others offer. Student writers no longer see their writing solely from a professor's viewpoint. Instead, 20, 30, or more people beyond the teacher read and respond to what the student has written. Students learn to look at their writing through the eyes of a larger, more diverse reading audience rather than through a single holistic number, essay grade, or letter grade given by an instructor This is a great achievement for the writing classroom, because it emphasizes all the ideas process writing purports. Maybe the reactions of dozens or hundreds of readers are more reliable and valid approaches to writing assessment than the models we now have in place. However, all of this does little to express to the powers that be in institutions just what the student did over the course of a semester. This is a particular problem for faculty or K–12 teachers functioning in an academic culture that requires grades and specific outcomes; a check or minus system applied to major projects or significant components of the writing class may not be a useful assessment tool even when a lack of intervention is the wisest choice. If internetworked writing courses or hybrid electronic or F2F writing courses are to demonstrate the power and potential for Composition's future, then there need to be some type of new or different evaluation mechanisms in place to accommodate student writing performed in public spaces so those who teach at institutions governed by learning outcomes, assessment goals, and other accountability concerns can address writing development when students engage in public writing situations.

For many writing instructors, making the move to internetworked writing assignments conflicts with institutional demands for accountability through high-stakes testing. Without a mechanism in place to gauge student learning, some school districts, like some colleges and universities, will not permit instructors or their writing programs to incorporate significant changes that encourage student writers to produce more of their assignments online. The dominant perception held by many legislators, administrators, and faculty is that without some form of high-stakes testing (barrier exams, large-scale performance portfolios, rising junior essays, etc.), standards cannot and will not be reinforced, instructors will not realize what is important to teach, and students will not be motivated to work harder to learn, and that the results of these tests provide better instruction for future students as well as offer better opportunities for the instructors' professional development (Amerin & Berliner, 2002).

How this belief affects online writing and its assessment connects to how we in Composition have tested writing. Unlike the five-paragraph model that produces predictable "rote writing" (Amerin & Berliner, 2002) and lends itself to holistic scoring, internetworked writing neither conforms to a single format nor reflects a predictable model. A rubric becomes highly unreliable if there is no consistent pattern in the genre. Often genuine electronic writing displays little consistent surface patterning or generic conventions. Consequently, many writing instructors find themselves in a curricular mismatch—the learning goals of the outcome test do not mesh with the critical skills needed to generate electronic texts. Worse yet, there is no consistent model to use to assess the students' work.

Even if writing faculties align the curriculum to include some e-texts, assessing them raises questions of efficiency The processing time for an instructor to evaluate a range of electronic texts can be enormous—how would an instructor be compensated for the additional hours needed to review this work? Although we can look to portfolio assessment, where the same question has been asked and not easily resolved in many places, the number and variety of electronic texts produced in a given semester just by one student can be enormous. Multiply this by 60 or 80 students in the three or four sections of composition a college instructor might teach, or the 125 students a high school teacher might reach, and the answer seems to be just to chuck the whole idea of integrating electronic writing assignments. At the end of a marking period, when grades are due and rapid feedback is necessary, who wants to shuffle more files—electronic or paper—than is absolutely needed?

The problem is that society and our students are devouring technology. As our culture becomes increasingly more information-dependent, students' futures depend on their facility with technology. It would be wrongheaded for Composition to retain 19th-century writing models and early 20th-century assessment plans in light of the rapid changes in writing and communication occurring in the world. As a field and as individual practitioners, we must incorporate more networked writing experiences into the curriculum. As networked writing becomes a greater part of the Composition curriculum, it becomes increasingly more important to have an assessment mechanism in place that measures students' work in this new medium. Otherwise, measuring students' writing is untenable, because part of the students' skill in writing is working with the medium. Therefore, it is time to reinvent Composition to account for the convergence between technology and assessment in the writing curriculum.

Can reinventing Composition solve the problems of poor student placement in our classes, the issues of the digital divide that separate students from different racial and socioeconomic backgrounds, and the rising concerns of student cheating and academic dishonesty, along with nearly 100 other local issues that plague writing pro-

grams? Probably not. However, we may be able to make some inroads into these areas by considering the best of the old ideas with
the promise of the new.

THE WRITING CLASSROOM AS SALON

Perhaps the first step in reinventing Composition needs to begin with
the classroom and teacher practices. For me, as for many other writing instructors, the classroom is the site where everything related to
the teaching of writing begins. Whether the class's location is in
cyberspace, in a brick-and-mortar building, or in some hybrid form
does not matter. What does matter is the link between a writing
teacher's classroom practices and the students' performance
(Wenglinsky, 2002). That is why to reinvent Composition in an age
of technological convergence, we must first reinvent the metaphor
used to describe the spaces in which we teach. The shift in meta-
phoric thinking then becomes a way to reexamine our teaching and
assessment practices in light of the rise of computer technology.

The writing classroom as salon arises from the life of Kenneth
Burke. Salons were extremely important in Burke's growth as a
young intellectual (Selzer, 1996). In the salon, people gather to exchange ideas. Like Burke did with his peers, young writers in the
classroom meet to share their beliefs, positions, aspirations, and
views related to topical material. Unlike the private or semiprivate
discussions students have with their instructors or peer groups in
current-traditional or process writing classes, in a salon format,
discussion and writing are made public, open to all.

When our words move from the private or semiprivate domain
of a papertext assignment into a public forum like a list or MOO or
a web page, students and their instructors must realize that language is in a free zone, a place that exceeds the boundaries of classroom, corporate, administrative, or legislative authority. It is also
a place where interested people feel motivated enough to respond
to what they read. The salon metaphor is used to describe this ex-
changing of ideas in the free zone. The salon is a fitting image for
what occurs in the online classroom experience, because it evokes
the historical understanding of the salon as a center of criticism
and debate with other similarly educated individuals. Through
ongoing interchanges of smart discourse and authentic reflection
with classmates and others via the computer network, students

develop lines of thinking and writing that embrace a wider range of ideas that what is often possible in the traditional classroom setting and what can be measured by conventional writing assessment methods.

Envisioning the writing classroom as a salon transforms the present structure of most composition classes in three distinct ways that jolt established writing assessment plans. First, computer technology alters the style, discussion climate, and topic considerations found in college writing classes. Instead of the course being teacher-centered or test-centered to maintain the talk–write balance, networked writing classes demand that students keep the discussions organized and going. Students now balance the talk–write schism. Depending on the classroom format, the possibility exists that even a write–write split occurs in asynchronous classes. This may make it difficult for teachers to select a workable topic prompt from which students are to write, because online conversations tend to be fragmented exchanges or threads that morph into new discussions. Second, to borrow from Jürgen Habermas (1991), a networked environment promotes social interplay that completely disregards one's status or rank. Instead of hierarchical or institutional structures granting participants the oppor- tunity to write or listen with authority, the salon format of online discussions leads the class to value authority based on the best arguments made in support of or in defense of an issue—whether the best argument is made by the students or the professor. This notion runs counter to holistic assessment, because it is up to the "trained" reader—usually a member of the writing faculty or a graduate student—to determine what is the proper argument for the prompt.

A third way that the salon metaphor highlights a change in the dynamics of classroom discussion is by including all students in the teaching mix as readers, respondents or spectators. The exclusion that happens in the Siberian outposts of traditional classroom spaces (corners, back rows, near windows, etc.) dissipates in the networked environment. In chat, integrated writing software programs, or other online activities, students must be attentive. Although some students may choose to stay silent or to redirect topics under discussion to something more to their liking, everyone is available to discuss the topics at hand. Rarely in assessment situations are students able to shift topic prompts to fit their interests. Closely linked to this behavior is the way the writing class becomes radicalized through

technology. When a student is writing in the public sphere of the salon, a student's innermost thoughts (his or her subjectivity) move
away from being exclusively "I centered" and move toward developing a greater sense of how others think about similar issues. This
process helps many students gain empathy and insight regarding a
topic that can be presented at the students' level. Through e-mail,
chat, or MOO exchanges, students offer private thoughts and question not only their thoughts but the thoughts of others as well. In
this process, critical reflection occurs, and students shape their views
around the contexts and audiences available to them. Again, the
question becomes, how do writing teachers measure this type of
critical development with the current writing assessment tools
available to them?

THE EFFECTS OF TECHNOLOGICAL CONVERGENCE
ON THE WRITING CLASSROOM

Not only does convergence recast the presentation of course content
and classroom dynamics in a composition class, convergence also
changes what compositionists teach as part of the writing process.
Writing for web space, hypertexts, weblogs, or MOOs, for instance,
requires teaching faculty to include lessons on visual rhetoric and
design to complete specific tasks. Adding the dimension of visual
rhetoric generates another layer of competency and complexity to a
student's work. Aside from the more common understanding of
what writing is for most composition courses—clarity and coherence, for example—instructors need to add the aspects of "creativity,
curiosity, consideration, and consistency" (Huntley & Latchaw,
1998, p. 108). As educational assessment specialists Joan Huntley
and Joan Latchaw noted, infusing the networked phases of the classroom with consideration—defined by the authors as "collegial respect" (1998, p. 108) for students—imparts a very different
classroom dynamic for assessment. Rather than construct an adversarial professor–student relationship in the writing class, consideration anticipates a cooperative, collaborative spirit of learning for
both the instructor and the students.

From my own experience over these last several years of teaching
writing in different computer-based class environments, it appears
that technology does reduce the antagonistic relationship between
instructor and student. This is in direct opposition to the rising an-

tagonisms created by standardized or traditional writing assessment methods. In varying degrees depending on the methods used, writing assessment frequently leans toward establishing conflict-filled relationships between professors and their students. Reducing the opposition between teacher and student is a radical step in changing the cultural climate of the Composition sequence at many colleges and universities. Once the hostility levels with students are decreased, however, the evaluation process becomes more difficult for the instructor. As the professor begins to view both herself and her students as writers working toward a goal in a given context, appraisals take on a different quality. No longer does the top-down dispensing of advice and grades hold in this new environment; rather, discussions about writing become a dialogic exchange between two or more writers. Treating students as colleagues in a writing experience dramatically challenges the identity-building process that usually occurs with the exit essay or final portfolio development. Instead of asking students to construct a false academic identity for their writing on a timed essay or in a reflective portfolio letter, computer-mediated writing invites students to compose assignments that correspond to various facets of the students' personalities. So, for e-mail, students may adopt creative pseudonyms like "bookworm" or "jiveturkey" or "blahblahblah25," whereas their web sites reflect more focused career or avocational interests that illustrate the students' curiosity. As a result, many instructors begin to see their students as complex, inventive rhetors who establish identities that fit specific discourse situations.

Although concepts like curiosity, creativity, and consideration are currently beyond the scope of writing assessment practices, as Huntley and Latchaw (1998) observed, these ideas are vitally important for strong online communication. These authors' research (Huntley & Latchaw, 1998) suggests that Composition needs to consider modifying its current assessment practices, not only to accommodate the cognitive changes in a writer's knowledge base when she composes electronically but also to adjust to the shift in the interpersonal relationships that writing teachers establish with their students.

ELECTRONIC WRITING AND THE IMPLICATIONS FOR ASSESSMENT

Writing in a public sphere like a classroom motivated by technological convergence alters what it means for compositionists to evaluate a piece of student writing. Past practices, such as indirect assessment and direct assessment featuring holistic scoring or primary trait analysis, allowed writing programs or instructors to create some type of consensus-driven, concrete criteria and apply them to a wide range of reading situations. This system worked well because the product, the exam or the essay, was developed by a single writer and reflected a single voice, usually that of the instructor. In the years ahead, as the synergy between computing and writing becomes complete, writing instructors and their programs will need to consider very different criteria for successful online composing than those used now. Eventually, writing teachers will have to measure interactivity, visuality, and aurality combined with writing in a truly authentic context like a web page or a blog. This future situation not only requires faculty to reconsider writing assessment and its implications when full computer convergence in Composition occurs; it also demands that Composition's culture begin to rethink what it means to be literate in a digital society. As the concept of literacy broadens in a digital environment to incorporate the use of information technologies, so must the concept of assessment be expanded if there is any hope of retaining validity in the evaluation process. Although the dilemma of validity arises in a later chapter, it is important early on for readers to begin thinking about the questions surrounding validity in computer-based classrooms that must have a writing assessment component.

The discussion of validity in writing assessment merged with computer technology is taken up in a later chapter. In this section, however, it is more important for us to explore the implications for writing assessment when convergence affects the evaluation process. First, we need to contemplate some general perceptions about writing assessment and how computer-based writing instruction explodes these impressions.

A standard yet simplistic description of writing assessment as many educators often define it was pulled from a current textbook on authentic literacy assessment:

> Composition is the interaction of the writer's knowledge, the text to be created, and the context within which writing occurs .... Specifically, the writer's knowledge consists of (1) knowledge of the writing process, (2) topic knowledge, (3) discourse knowledge (knowledge of text structures, such as narrative, expository, persuasive), (4) vocabulary knowledge, (5) interest in writing, (6) motivation to write, and (7)

knowledge of linguistic devices (techniques writers use to help reader make connections among ideas). In addition, writing is also affected by the writer's command of production components, such as handwriting, spelling, and punctuation. (Leslie & Jett-Simpson, 1997, p.19)

Few in Composition would argue with the opening line of these authors' description of composition, regardless of our pedagogical inclinations. Generally, writing instructors of any persuasion would agree that the writing process depends on how writers interact with what they know, the genre, and the situation in which they are writing. However, given the vast amount of research done in the writing process over the last 30 years, Leslie and Jett-Simpson's oversimplification of what comprises "writer's knowledge" in their definition is astounding. If the composing process were as easily defined and classified as these authors suggest—even in a F2F writing class—evaluating a student writer's progress would not be the painstaking event it frequently seems to be for writing faculty each semester. What these authors (and those who subscribe to this understanding of composition in the field of tests and measurements) fail to acknowledge is each of these reductive categories is highly mediated and negotiated by the texts students produce and the contexts in which students produce those texts, as Composition has discovered over the last 3 to 5 decades. Yet what Leslie and Jett-Simpson (1997) proffered in their basic, but problematic, definition is an all-too-common one guiding both the assessment of student writing at the college level and the definition of assessment used by hundreds of writing instructors and their program administrators. This definition of writing assessment is the one most subject to transformation in Composition's convergence with technology.

A writer's knowledge in networked spaces is quite different from what is presented in the Leslie and Jett-Simpson (1997) model. Christina Haas (1996) noted that the student writer must adapt to the material changes in the writing process caused by computer technology. Writers plan, write, and revise differently when word processing compared with pen-and-paper production. For instance, Haas (1996) explained that studies indicate writers may do less higher level text planning (organization, thesis development, and decisions about tone or rhetorical selections) with the computer. Instead, writers may focus more on low-level text planning (surface level error) because small computer screens constrain the writer from seeing the entire text and direct the writer to think in smaller text pieces. Moreover, students who are unskilled or un-comfortable with text manipulation (cut and paste) or mouse dex-terity may also feel physically distant from the text, which can also affect their writing (Haas, 1996). So, as Carol Sweedler Brown dis-covered in 1991 with her work on typed versus handwritten as-sessment essays, textual production looks much different to the writer and the reader; compared with handwritten papers, com-puter-processed texts are shorter and the graphic appearance of computer text affects readers' decisions.

Consequently, in holistic assessment situations, whether con-ducted under single essay or portfolio conditions, the student writer must have an added dimension of knowledge in the writing process when using a computer: He or she must have facility with how computer technology works to present a clear, understandable presentation as well as to construct a concise message. This knowl-edge of how technology integrates with writing expands greatly when students move away from word processing and toward mul-timedia presentations like web sites, hypertexts, or MOOs. Even if students compose something as simple as e-mail on the computer, the writer's knowledge of technology and how it can affect the writing process increases beyond simple word processing.

Leslie and Jett-Simpson (1997) suggested that topic knowledge is important for student writers to demonstrate in an assessment. To a degree this is also true in computer-based writing assignments. However, what becomes more critical for students' topic knowledge is how the writers can pace the flow of information for their audi-ences as well as recognizing the ways in which students can create messages of importance and interest for their audience. Additionally, students demonstrating topic knowledge in networked writing sometimes become mediated by the incorporation of an aesthetically complex presentation of their work, such as producing multimedia web sites or MOO structures. Often, though, writing in these newer electronic environments depends on students drawing on collabora-tive efforts to write a MOO or lines of HTML code. So, how writing instructors define "topic knowledge" in assessment has to evolve from an understanding of how collaboration enhances a writer's grasping the topic as well as his or her performance. Thus, a shift in writing assessment must happen because instructors have to move from evaluating the finished product to evaluating what students do along the way in completing a project.

Perhaps no area in writing assessment will be affected more by technological convergence than discourse knowledge. The standard expository modes of discourse explode under the weight of multimedia and polyvocality that exist in computer-assisted writing instruction. Although stories about human experiences, polemics, fantasies, poems, advertising, and talk remain in networked environments, the messages look much different compared with their papertext counterparts. In computer-mediated communication and converged space, these genres blur as writers combine forms to create new hybrid genres to communicate with their audiences. Improvisation and innovation instead of prescribed textbook limitations spur the rhetorical choices a writer makes in electronically produced writing.

Furthermore, writing assessment usually depends on students matching—or trying to match—specific conventions in their writing that are defined by a program's writing faculty or a college or university as being critical to certify one's literacy. The more proficiently students can match their writing to the desired conventions, the better the score they receive on the exit portfolio or barrier essay. The more (or less, depending on the result) a student can model a particular style of writing, the easier it is to certify the student as part of a literate college or university population. If Composition is to move further into computer-based writing instruction, this discourse game must change. Rhetorical and linguistic improvisation or innovation—so desirable in networked writing—resists standardization, which puts students highly involved in computer-based writing classes at some risk for strong performance in the usual battery of writing assessment tests that measure traditional generic structures or usage. Cheryl Forbes pointed to this dilemma in her 1996 *Computers and Composition* article on overriding and overwriting student work. Even when teachers use what Composition considers to be a more humane, more performative assessment tool, the portfolio, Forbes (1996) addressed the potential for writing teachers to overwrite students' decisions in electronic compositions by inserting lengthy teacher comments, by using bold or heavy text fonts in strong colors to emphasize teacher comments to students, or by interrupting or even adding sentences to the students' work.

Equally restrictive is the present batch of holistic essay-grading software designed to take the "subjectivity" out of teacher essay evaluation. If such programs eventually were to be extended to networked writing assignments for the sake of grading efficiency, there would be significant difficulties beyond what compositionists already have found. Given the fluid nature of writing in hypertext, MOO, or other electronic environments, how will the software package discern when an error is an error or when the "mistake" is a rhetorical or linguistic improvisation designed to play to an audience beyond the teacher? There is far more rhetorical and linguistic play in electronic communication, and the current predicate analysis or key-word-in-context formats used by these software programs are unable to make these "subjective" decisions in papertext situations.

Moreover, because of the multiple contexts available to a reader or writer in electronic texts, how does the computer program distinguish which contexts are appropriate for the material under review? Even a live instructor holistically reading an electronic text is weighed down with problems if she is using the typical rubric generated to read written essays. Although it is used in many ways, the holistic model is best used for short expository essays written under very specific conditions. Holistic essay scoring certainly was never designed for use with public texts. Although certain fields, like public relations and advertising, use various readability scales, like the Gunning-Fog Index or Flesch's scale, to determine how reader-friendly a text is, these gauges do little to help students improve their writing beyond isolating surface constructions.

Still other questions emerge when we explore how traditional writing assessment tools could function in a networked writing environment. How can an individual teacher argue with colleagues to build a consensus if she is reading a set of electronic texts without wrenching authority from the student writer who understands the community for which he writes? How can that same individual teacher set all the correct parameters for the machine's reading of that student's electronic text? If one of the purposes for Composition is to move students into taking more authorial stances in their writing through public reception of their work, then machine reading of students' electronic work clearly runs counter to that purpose—regardless of how efficient some may believe the evaluation process may be.

A further concern compositionists should have about the use of current writing assessment tools being used for students' electronic communication centers on issues of who controls the text. Because these various writing and essay-grading software packages make the possibility of wresting control from the student writer so much easier for the teacher, as Forbes' article (1996) illustrates, composition practitioners may need to return to thinking about writing as an art and assessing writing much like one does a painting or a sculpture. This, particularly, may be an effective way of discussing networked texts—especially for those e-texts that incorporate multimedia or polyvocality that cut against the grain of academic or professional norms. Instead of measuring optimal competence in a given setting (as is the case with holistic evaluation) or longitudinally for a series of genres (portfolio or webfolio use), electronic texts could be considered and evaluated in terms of their communicative context. That is, how does the message express a point clearly and interestingly to an audience, and how does the writer use the tools and techniques available to him or her in various combinations to relate that message to the audience? In this assessment model, evaluators examine the writing in context to see how it functions aesthetically, argumentatively, conceptually, and performatively as well as structurally for that community. What communicative assessment asks of instructors is to reorient the process of evaluating students' writing from being success-oriented (i.e., grade or score-driven) toward developing an understanding of how e-texts function in various contexts.

A very real possibility for changing the focus in online writing assessment to acknowledge public, communicative criteria is that students' divergent thinking and problem-solving abilities can be rewarded instead of ignored or undervalued, as they so often are now in traditional assessment methods. Currently, if Michael Williamson's (Huot & Williamson, 1993) observation still holds true, writing specialists do not have any way of assessing written discourse that exceeds the fixed boundaries of academic writing. Williamson (Huot & Williamson, 1993) noted that a major deficit of either indirect or direct writing assessment models is that creative, divergent thinking is not encouraged; rather, conforming to an academic norm is stressed. Following Williamson's line of thought, then, the implication of a communicative form of writing assessment means compositionists must recognize that a linguistic community is not identical for all participants and that different communities depend on different interpretive systems. This is an important point for evaluating electronic communication, because individuals frequently maintain various levels of investment and expertise in a topic under discussion. In these instances, students' discursive acumen turns on complex reasoning to draw out the shared sentiments to a diverse group of writers and thinkers, particularly if third-party participants (not the course instructor or classmates) become involved in the reading of the text.

Therefore, a change must happen in the ways in which compositionists assess e-texts in the writing classroom. Written discourse shaped by computer technology requires instructors to return to Composition's rhetorical roots to find a language and a methodology to evaluate e-texts. A reintroduction of terms like *kairos*, *copia*, *expediency*, and *techne* becomes important to represent different applications of how student writers manipulate language and text to respond to their global audiences. These terms offer instructors a name for the types of intended effects that occur in an electronically produced text as well as for those that occur in papertext formats. To assess students' use of these concepts in the context of an electronic text, though, one needs to be attentive not only to how well student writers address situational time, linguistic and argumentative facility, and community values but also to the art of offering all this information in a productive way (*techne*).

Techne is a critical criterion for evaluating the communicative worth of e-texts, because it reflects the writers' ability to handle typography, graphics, color, white or blank space, and even sound in addition to the students' competence with the written word. Intentionally or not, writers who misapply techne by incorrectly selecting hyperlinks, audio, fonts, graphics, color, background colors, or white space may not understand or recognize a certain community's values for clarity or coherence in navigation or design. In networked writing, students and instructors must be aware that clarity and coherence extend beyond the sentences on screen. For a web page, a hypertext story, or any other form of online writing, the entire context becomes a communicative act, and all aspects of the genre have to work in concert for the item to be considered meaningful.

Thus, in networked writing contexts, missteps grounded in techne can affect a writer's argumentative eloquence, as the audience's attention moves from the point of argument to a series of running Java applets, clashes between background and font colors, unreadable typefaces, or nonfunctioning links or commands. This is why writing specialists need to reconsider electronic writing assessment in terms of aesthetic criticism. The merging of the visual and the verbal in an e-text demands that instructors contemplate both the rhetorical effect beyond the written word and the volume of knowledge a writer must possess to create functioning MOOs, web sites, multimedia presentations, hypertexts, and so on. Consequently, the standardized, oversimplified understanding of writing assessment outlined by Leslie and Jett-Simpson (1997) earlier in this chapter should not apply to online writing assignments. Something else, some other criteria, must be developed to account for writing done in networked environments. This "something else" will be taken up in detail in the following chapters.

"Video killed the radio star," so the Buggles' 1980 song goes, but the trends in technological convergence depend too heavily on the written word for Composition and its practitioners to vanish. For computers not to kill the composition teacher, it is increasingly more important for writing instructors to be well trained technologically and assessment-savvy—ready to teach in whatever configurations future composition classrooms take. Convergence can become a way for Composition and its specialists to speak authoritatively about writing in a digital age and to move out of the literal and figurative academic basement it has dwelled in for more than a century. However, before Composition asserts its voice in local or large-scale settings, there need to be some mechanisms in place to assess writing that arises from internetworked classes. As most university faculties realize, the state legislatures that govern higher education now expect outcomes assessment for most courses, but particularly so for anything connected to student literacy. In fact, the 2004 State of the Union speech hinted that the No Child Left Behind Act would be extended to grades 13 through 20, and many states' legislatures suggest that it is time for public colleges to be held accountable for student learning, as is the recent State University of New York Regents' decision to have testing models in place to gauge student learning in writing. Having electronically scored 20-minute essays is not equivalent to the more complex and demanding nature of internetworked writing, which is becoming the foundation for the type of writing many students face in their future professions.

Although electronic portfolios are a start toward college instructors documenting student growth and accountability in writing, as

Kathleen Blake Yancey (1999) recognized, newer technology and more experienced students will require writing programs to have other assessment procedures in place to evaluate these noncanonical e-texts. How and why these fresher methods develop are yet to be seen, but we can look to what Composition now knows about computer-based writing instruction, digital literacy, technology redefining the text, and writing assessment to move into the next phase.

Chapter 2

Transforming Texts, Transforming Assessment

A text and what student writers do with the production of a text are always at the center of writing instruction and assessment, regardless of the medium used. Similarly, the preconceptions that writing faculty maintain about what a text is and how it should look influence how student texts are received. Nowhere do these two ideas emerge more clearly than when writing faculty engage in the assessment of student-produced electronic texts. In her essay, "The Effect of Hypertext of Processes of Reading and Writing," Davida Charney (1994) observed that "our conception of text as an orderly succession of ideas is strongly reinforced by the constraints of the standard print medium: texts come to us on printed pages that we generally read in order, from the top down and from left to right" (p. 238). The order that most faculty members have come to know is changing, however. As networked writing becomes more prevalent in the college composition classroom, the definition and nature of what a text is and what writers can do with texts are shifting. We are no longer bound to the constraints of the print medium. This point is important as computers increasingly affect the teaching of writing and the call to assess e-texts becomes greater.

Guenther Kress, in *Page to Screen* (in Snyder, 1998), pointed us toward the direction writing is taking in internetworked environments when he wrote: "With convergence of technologies (telephone, television, radio, computer), competence in all modes of representation will simply be assumed—even though what is assumed may not in fact be available" (p. 57). Until that time in society when technological convergence occurs to such a degree that all writers will have an assumed

29

competence in writing and thinking in cyberspace, compositionists not only will have to design curricula that account for teaching students how to become electronically and informationally literate but will also have to create assessment practices that explain how student writers develop and master the multimodal abilities needed to be considered literate. This suggests that writing specialists need to address the textual, design, and writing process variations between electronic texts and papertexts as well as the transformations that must take place in writing assessment to accommodate the shifts in texts, design needs, and composing processes.

Writing faculty can see the textual differences between paper and pixel almost immediately in the look and structure of electronic texts. E-texts vary greatly from traditional, stand-alone papertexts in obvious ways. However, what many compositionists may not realize is that seven characteristics distinguish e-texts from their paper cousins. These characteristics clearly affect how a student writer approaches the task of creating an electronic work:

- Length. E-texts are typically short; usually a few paragraphs at the most. A 1,000-word essay on a web site reads like a long novel, sometimes like a very bad long novel.
- Processing information. Readers of e-texts do not read carefully. Most scan or skim data to mine nuggets of information. Generally, e-text readers spend 60 seconds or less scanning a page of web content. Reading in this manner affects how people process information.
- Style. Bulleted lists, clear graphics, active voice, and minimalist sentences that are hard-crafted are preferred over long, developed narratives or academic prose. Also, the subtleties of print are missed or ignored in e-textual spaces. Writers in inter-networked environments aim for a lively style that goes for immediate effect.
- Wit. Clever, snappy, and quick phrasings hold e-text readers' interest. This is particularly critical when constructing hyperlinks that lead readers to additional information. Humor is appreciated and encouraged, unlike in most of academic writing.
- Purpose. The idea and the goal of the e-text must be conjoined for it to be successful. All visuals, navigation tools, or bars, as well as the content, have to work together to generate a desired effect on the reader.

- Editing. Editing is a critical stage in the production of e-texts. Not only must long sentences be pared down to their essences, but errors have to be reduced so as not to interfere with the content or become magnified on screen.
- Cross-trained skills. Effective e-text writers need to be competent in their use of a number of electronic genres (such as lists, MOOs, and web pages or e-mail) and software programs (such as Photoshop, Adobe PDF, Java, Flash, and HTML or its equivalent in FrontPage or Dreamweaver). Writers cross-trained in the various e-genres and tools become cognizant of what design and content issues arise for readers and the expectations readers have for obtaining information.

One way for composition specialists to consider the changes a writer must make to adapt to new media writing is to first think about the levels of rhetorical sophistication that students need to develop. Unlike papertexts, where crafting words and phrases elicits various audience responses, with e-texts the students must also layer graphics and design into the text so they can gain an immediate effect. Anyone who has watched students directly import a paper written for a class assignment to a web site recognizes a thoughtless use of bandwidth. In these instances, the student's paper is too long for readers to navigate easily or to absorb. Additionally, other problems exist. The ideas and the goal of that web page are unclear, and the academic style of most class papers is a mismatch for the lighter, more informative tones of an e-text.

In internetworked spaces, student writers have multiple opportunities to select and blend genres and techniques beyond those that occur in print formats. Yet students are also constrained by the design tools and the stylistic concerns that affect a reader's experience of viewing type on screen. It is this broad scope of electronic textual possibilities and the ability for an e-text to cross over into one or more textual genres that offer the immediate differences between networked and non-networked texts. It is also what confounds writing teachers in their evaluation of an e-text. E-text genres range from e-mail postings to complex hyperlinked (Hypertext) stories and articles to student-developed web pages grounded in a research topic or an electronic portfolio that traces a semesters, a year's, or an entire college career's worth of work. This is not to mention other e-texts, like MOOs or weblogs, which blend text and cyberspace.

What grounds these various e-texts is Joan Tornow's (1997) important observation that e-texts, particularly e-mail threads, are "heavily context-dependent, yet the exact referent may not be immediately evident" (p. 73). Tornow's point underscores the more extensive and sophisticated coverage that the e-mail genre in the classroom space has received from computer and composition specialists. But what can be said for e-mail also extends to the other e-texts as well—these genres are highly context-dependent compared with most papertexts; however, the differences may not always be instantly apparent to the instructor.

Frequently this situation arises with student web pages, which some writing instructors erroneously compare to student papers. These teachers often do not realize that the change from paper to pixel creates a shift in the students' writing processes, particularly in the editing processes. Kathryn Sutherland's essay collection, *The Electronic Text* (1998), extends this idea in greater depth as contributors explain how e-texts require different editing activities compared with their papertext counterparts. In the same vein, Christina Haas (1996) also identified numerous differences in writers' composing processes when the material tools used for writing change.

Undoubtedly, a critical mass exists in the computer and composition literature that outlines the distinctions between writing on screen and on paper. Without retracing all of these authors' steps, this chapter explores how technological convergence's transformation of the text sets in motion a transformation both in what writers can do with electronic texts and in what instructors can do with writing assessment. This is an important next step in the convergence process taking place within Composition. It is not enough anymore in higher education just to argue that a new form of writing and texts exists. In an era of learning outcomes, assessment, and both being tied to budgets and faculty hires, one must also be able to measure how student writing grows and develops in the internetworked classroom. Moreover, if Composition truly values the teaching of writing through the use of computers, then it is imperative that individuals in Composition Studies offer assessment models to evaluate the work students (and their teachers) do in the classroom. Otherwise, as Edward White (1994) warned, people outside of Composition will do the evaluating for us.

The field has learned enough about computers for compositionists to recognize that technology has modified the characteristics of a text and textual production. Now, though, writing instructors need to explore how these transformations in the text can be assessed if they are to respond with any type of authority to institutional and student demands. External oppositional voices—and some internal antagonistic voices as well—are able to dismiss any curricular innovation like technological convergence or even Composition itself if there is a lack of correspondence between the stated course goals or standards and the ability to measure the students' capability for meeting them. The computer decentralizes the teacher's classroom authority and redistributes it throughout a roomful of writers, thereby removing much of the traditional writing teacher's direct intervention in the overall evaluation of students' writing. That is why greater efforts need to be made to demonstrate to the naysayers that course goals, standards, and outcomes can and do exist for these new textual forms. Mechanisms need to be in place to show administrators, faculty, and students that e-texts can be appraised in some way and can show student growth in writing.

As more writing programs and their professors enter the brave new world of program assessment at the same time that campus administrators and accreditation groups are encouraging greater use of technology in composition classes, the integration of writing assessment and computer technology has to be examined carefully. All of us have to ask ourselves whether writing instructors can evaluate written work that is completely "owned" by the students, especially if the entire class develops into its own literate learning community and so understands the language, the contexts, and the adaptability of the discourse to communicate with others. Or, is Composition such the example that classroom-generated writing—especially in assessment contexts—will never be fully "owned" by student writers and will always have, to varying degrees, the teacher overriding or overwriting the final submission?

Textual ownership is a central and sensitive issue in computer-based writing assessment, because students who upload any electronic texts to the Internet are publishing authors and share the same rights and privileges to their written work that their professors do. Just as many writing teachers bristle at moderated listowners who assess and overwrite submitted posts before distributing them to the audience, student writers involved in networked writing spaces find themselves equally piqued when writing teachers engage in these practices. If writing instructors are teaching students how to craft messages for a public audience, and then the teacher over-rides or overwrites student work designed for a specific Internet audience, what does it teach the student? Moreover, when assessment practices infringe on the students' writing for a global audience, even when the materials are produced for a class, which holds more sway—the assessment mechanism or the audience?

Before I attempt to answer these questions in later chapters, it is important to examine the critical element for transforming our present theories of writing assessment in the age of technological convergence: the text. In Composition, we regularly think of the text as *the Text*—something singular, even if written collaboratively, and enduring—the "finished" product of multiple drafts and revisions. Yet this is a very isolated understanding of what a text is and what it can do for electronic communication. Technological convergence alters this older, print-driven expectation of what a text is. In convergence, writers use and combine different media to communicate similar ideas and goals. Depending on a writer's techniques, limitations, and language ability and selected media technologies, a text can become highly fluid and obscure those characteristics that many writing instructors have come to associate with the idea of *the Text*, that is, the feeling of bookishness (Haas, 1996) that a traditional papertext format presents to a reader.

Through the influences of poststructural and postmodern theory, numerous compositionists recognize that writers shape texts along multiple social, political, gendered, economic, racial, and aesthetic lines. To some degree, these newer theoretical lines help us to reduce the bookishness that exists in more traditionally written texts, because these ideas suggest that even the most solidly written article or book maintains points of fracture and disjunction that allow us to unravel the text's meanings. However, even the most experimental or unraveled papertext still conforms to enough conventions for instructors to make some kind of informed judgment on the work in front of them. This is because, as Gunther Kress indicated in his work *Writing the Future*, there are three distinct textual categories in the English curriculum that govern our decisions on how to approach a text:

- The culturally salient text
- The aesthetically valued (and valuable) text
- The mundane text (1994, p. 34)

These textual categories become central for our understanding of how instructors' knowledge of writing assessment corresponds to the text and how any given transformation in the text or in textual production changes the relation between writing assessment and text.

If we look first at the culturally salient text, the dominant criterion for its success is that of how significant the text is for specific cultural groups as well as for society at large. As Kress (1994) explained, a text's cultural salience depends on how well a piece of writing speaks to the cultural and social histories that exist and how it considers the possible cultural and social futures to come. The text's importance comes not from aesthetic or skill qualities but from how well the writer understands how his or her writing fits in with the concerns of a particular segment of society by adopting the language and rhetorical practices of that group. The culturally salient text, then, corresponds quite comfortably with the positions found in the social constructivist view of writing instruction. In this composing theory, a writer's competence is assessed by how satisfactorily he or she grasps the exigencies involved in an issue and by the degree to which the student writer uses language directed toward a particular audience to respond to a set of stakes.

Salience is not a primary issue with the second textual category, although the culture and politics of an era may determine what a dominant group finds beautiful or pleasing in a text. The aesthetically valued or valuable text, Kress (1994) suggested, reflects the merit that a group ascribes to a particular writing style. The aesthetically valued text category meshes well with Faigley, Cherry, and Jolliffe's description of the "literary view of composing" (1986, p. 13) reflected in some faculty members' approach to assessment. Together, these two positions propose a belief that there is an absolute sublime element in worthy texts, even in student texts, albeit it is an unteachable beauty—a grandness that readers must experience and writers must probe for through the writing process.

The mundane text is the most problem filled for writing assessment and for theories of composing. Yet the mundane text plays the greatest role in networked writing. For these reasons, I will spend a greater amount of time and space covering this textual category compared with the other two. Kress (1994) described mundane texts as those that "form the bedrock of social and economic life" (p. 38). The everyday forms of professional or occupational writing reflect mundane texts. From e-mail memos to Internet relay chat to interoffice papertext communications to flyers for used books on sale at the off-campus bookstore or an apartment rental, the mundane text must be understood by a wide audience. These texts are highly context-dependent. This occurs because a single, closed-minded account of what transpires is not always readily available. As Kress noted, mundane texts engage us in change, as "the pace of change, and the linguistic resources—a full knowledge of grammar, a deep understanding of text and the forms of texts … will be essential … to write the text that [writers] both need and wish to write in a time of perplexing uncertainties" (1994, p. 39, brackets mine). Therefore, readers and writers of mundane texts must cue into certain verb structures, deixis, or noun–pronoun references. To reach the widest audience possible, writers of mundane texts hope to draw on a panoply of accounts based on multiple and distinct social positions.

When the mundane text moves into computer-mediated writing instruction through the use of e-mail, chat, lists, web pages, weblogs, or hypertext or hypercard products, even more fragmentation of the single coherent sentence can occur. Instead of the standard subject–predicate constructions so familiar to written discourse, networked mundane texts shatter all expectations. These e-texts replace standard written discourse forms with iconography (emoticons, capitalized letters to indicate shouting, jpeg or gif images, or some of the more clever ASCII-generated signature files or V-cards), acronyms, hybridized grammatical structures that blend standard and phonetic discourse, or repetitious short postings of agreement that show support for the original poster's viewpoint (the "ditto" message). This type of fragmentation in a text ruptures the aesthetically valued sensibilities that many writing instructors develop during the course of their studies. Ditto messages, acronyms, and other common e-text elements may also disturb those who demand cultural salience in their writing. Consequently, instructors who hold too strongly to these textual categories often find themselves lamenting the laxity of networked writing.

However, rather than occurring because of student laziness or the use of some unconventional shorthand, some of the e-textual conventions listed here arise because the student writers are clearly aware of who will be writing and reading these texts. These readers are immediate in the sense that they are in the same room or same course as the writer. The context dependency in e-mail that Tornow described (Tornow, 1997) permits the use of mundane texts and alternative conventions because students do not have to imagine an "ideal" reader or writer. Nor do the students have to imagine the assumptions these readers and writers have, although misinterpretation of a writer's statement can and does occur. As a result, students are cognizant of the relationships they wish to form online. In turn, as each class interacts on a discussion list, for instance, not only does a community of writers form, but specific discursive rules for that class arise. Misinterpretations generally happen when one student applies the discourse rules from one class to another. It seems that the context dependency of the class postings does not permit discourse rules to transfer across contexts. Violations of the established rules of discourse for the class are frequently met with assorted flames, silence, or questions for the violators to clarify their positions.

As threads multiply, instructors familiar with electronic communication notice that written collaboration begins as well, as students (and sometimes the instructor) contribute ideas to, delete unwanted information from, and alter their positions across a discussion. If instructors follow the patterns of conversation, intelligent discussions emerge through the associations and connections each writer makes with others by sharing his or her individual views instead of following prescriptive rules for writing to an audience or to a genre.

Another significant part of the mundane text, especially as it pertains to networked writing environments, is the medium in which the writer produces the text. For instance, in popular culture and in many academic journal articles, computers are often mythologized as being a "transparent" medium. Because most of the current software programs simulate familiar objects (files, folders, pieces of flying paper, document icons, file cabinets, etc.) rather than command lines of computer code, some people assume that users can see how a program works in its physical structure. Most computer users in the academy, even fairly sophisticated ones, find the machine itself and its inner workings are nearly impossible to comprehend; few actually know how a CPU processes data or how a network sends data packets of information. Even fewer care how the computer functions as long as when they boot up the system all parts are in working order. Unless one is writing on an older iMac and can see the lights and wires flickering under the shell, visually a computer is a fairly opaque thing compared with pen and paper.

Transparency, then, is a double-edged term: Transparency can mean either completely visible or invisible, depending on the user's point of reference. This same idea can be applied to computer-mediated texts and writing assessment. On the surface, with the computer, a text and a student's writing process may appear visible to the instructor, yet are writing teachers sure of what they see? And if writing instructors are not sure of what they see, how can they ever evaluate what students produce?

A mundane text can also be considered transparent in that, politically, the agenda or the ideas one has are fully visible to the audience, often as frequently as the political message occurs in the culturally salient text. However, the composing process of the mundane text, especially on a networked system, may be considered transparent in a different sense because the inner dynamics of writing—the planning, drafting, revising, adding of graphics if on a web site—are generally invisible for both the writer and the instructor even though the text is quite visible. Pamela Takayoshi at the University of Louisville noted in 1996 that through cut-and-paste techniques, computers create a "seamless flow of text" in composing that "dissolv[es] distinct segments of writing processes" (p. 245) for a writer. Consequently, with this new transparent medium compositionists find themselves working in a state of in/visibility. For every element of the writing that instructors see, there are distinct sections of the writing process that become hidden.

If instructors add hypertext or hyperlinked writing to the online classroom composing activities, then the transparency of the text is made even more in/visible in the process. The visibility of the nonlinear aspects of writing and reading hypertexts increases with the webbed structures. Likewise, the in/visibility of the writer's processes is established by the reader's decisions to select links in any order—unless, of course, the writer deliberately locks in the linkages to follow a particular path. So, if a writer chooses to, she could replicate standard textual conventions in hypertextual writing situations. This would make writing assessment easier for the instructor. But, this process defeats the idea of multivocality and nonlinearity inherent in cyberspace and merely reproduces a conventional text structure on screen. Moreover, assessing a hypertext or hyperlinked document in the same manner as a papertext clearly misses the full rhetorical, situational, and contextual elements of a student's work.

Therefore, the malleability of the mundane text makes it an excellent form for internetworked writing. As Takayoshi (1996) explained, even a simple piece of prose becomes a seamless production for a writer. Moreover, on screen, the mundane text becomes a vexing process for a writer. Compare Takayoshi's idea with psychologist Sherry Turkle's following observation about writing on a computer:

> Why is it so hard for me to turn away from the screen?... I feel pressure from a machine that seems itself to be perfect and leaves no one and no other thing but me to blame. It is hard for me to walk away from a not-yet-proofread text on the computer screen. In the electronic writing environment in which making a correction is as simple as striking a delete key, I experience a typographical error not as a mere slip of attention, but as a moral carelessness, for who could be so slovenly as not to take the one or two seconds to make it right? The computer tantalizes me with its holding power ... the promise that if I do it right, *it* will do it right, and right away. (1999, pp. 29–30)

Turkle's reflection on her own composing processes with the computer raises serious questions for the writing process and the production of a text as Composition has defined them over the last 30 years. As Takayoshi (1996) pointed out, students' self-awareness of the text's various stages of completeness has often been distinguished by what she calls "traditional markers"—paper copies that signify each stage of brainstorming, drafting, revising, and submitting the final product (p. 250). When traditional markers disappear or become transparent because a writer changes the medium from papertext to screen, as Turkle indicated, he or she must now reconsider when a text is still in need of revision and when it might be considered finished.

From what Turkle described, however, the computer creates a feeling in the writer that the conversation is never quite complete. Therefore, the student and the writing teacher must chart new ways of developing textual awareness for producing online compositions without the traditional markers to guide them—even for those workaday assignments that lead to larger projects or academic research.

THE CHARACTERISTICS OF A TRANSFORMED TEXT

Earlier in the chapter I made mention that many writing instructors see little distinction between students writing with pen and paper and with the computer. For these folks, writing is writing, regardless of the medium. Also, for these same instructors, assessing an e-text is a process akin to evaluating an exit essay or portfolio. This is not a view I share. As I see the situation, technological convergence transforms the idea of what a text is in four distinct ways that affect writing assessment:

1. Interactively
2. Graphically
3. Perspectively
4. Theoretically

Theorists, writing scholars, and practitioners over the last decade have argued successfully that e-texts have greater interactivity than their paper cousins. In response to this claim, many in Composition Studies nod their heads in agreement or cock their heads in skepticism. Few, though, question what interactivity is and how it distinguishes e-texts from conventional paper texts. Writing specialists need to more carefully (and critically) understand the interactive capability of e-texts so they can focus on how assessment should be modified for an age when students will compose regularly in a digital format.

Independent researcher Paul Gilster advanced a good, clear explanation of interactivity in his book *Digital Literacy* (1997). Whether one visits or authors web sites, hypertexts, or MOOs, interactivity is what allows a reader or a writer to "influence the way a particular situation is handled" and to "choose your own path through the site" (Gilster, 1997, p. 138). But, as Gilster suggested and compositionists should also consider, interactivity additionally refers to the mental processes writers must possess to construct a networked document (1997, p. 139).

In electronic environments, then, writers must learn new rhetorical strategies and techniques (*techne*) to create shorter, often more fragmented but still interconnected pieces that comprise a larger work. This process currently differs greatly from how most compositionists recognize the unfolding of the writing process in academic writing. To illustrate this point, here is a familiar example for most writing instructors. A 10- or 15-page student research paper is a fixed object. The student gathers her research in some manner, compiles it in a prescribed order, word processes it, revises or edits a draft, and turns in a sheaf of paper. The instructor may skim sections, focus on specific subsections, or read other sections with greater interest. Generally, the instructor reads the product in a linear manner. On completing the paper's reading, the professor develops a judgment about the student writer's competence based on the language of a discipline or of an argument. The professor bases her evaluation on the textual structures and conventions she has internalized throughout her studies and her research, much like Kress (1994) described in his outlining of the genres found in the English curriculum.

However, if the student writes a hypertext or webbed research work, once the student gathers the information, she has no prescribed order in which to place the evidence. To compensate for the computer's small screen and lack of strict spatial boundaries to mark page breaks, the student writer must think differently when organizing her material. Instead of writing long blocks of text that fill the computer screen and strain readers' eyes, as she might do in her papertext assignment, the student writer now considers constructing smaller data packets or chunks that are more reader-friendly. The student may decide to connect various ideas together or show the relation between specific events or characters using a hyperlink. To support her claim beyond her printed text, the student writer can incorporate photographs, video clips, sound, and line art. Now the student is writing interactively, drawing on multiple media to conjoin with her argument through the hyperlinking of external authorities, images, or sounds to engage the reader in a fuller discussion of the topic. In this situation the student is thinking and writing in a process that is completely different from what she would in a papertext system. Likewise, to receive and respond to this type of interactive writing, an instructor must reconfigure her ideas about textual structures, conventions, and organization to match the student writer's shift in medium.

Hyperlinks are sometimes considered as being digitized footnotes in an e-text. Although this is a familiar-sounding metaphor for some, it is an inaccurate observation. As Gilster (1997) suggested, a footnote narrows the discussion by offering readers a precise addition to an idea. Hyperlinks function in the opposite manner. They broaden the conversation by providing an extensive look at an idea. The result of a student's hyperlinked e-text is that the instructor, as reader, can enter the student's discussion from any number of places within the text, not necessarily at the linearly generated beginning, and glean different meanings from the student's writing and linking. Each reading and rereading requires the instructor to decide again how to grade the work in front of him or her.

This point leads to the problem of visuality that seeps into e-text, particularly in mundane texts that have wide audience appeal. Pamela Takayoshi (1996) rightly noted that Composition, as a field of study, has not fared well in deliberating the visual impact of a text on a reader in first-year composition classes; generally, visual rhetoric is addressed in professional writing classes or in advanced composition classes. That practice has to change as more first-year writing classes add inter-networked writing activities to the classroom and more first-year college students come prepared to write in networked classes.

Therefore, the writing process in first-year comp, although seamless in networked environments, now needs to account for student writers' visual rhetorical acumen as well as for their grasp of traditional rhetorical strategies. As we are all aware, graphics are central in much of electronic communication as part of its interactivity. Therefore, in internetworked writing, a writer's ability and skill to comprehend and create effective visual structures reflect the level to which a writer can recognize how the interplay of writing and image exists in cyberspace. These graphical elements are just as important to learn in first-year composition as the rhetorical modes in paper-text writing. Yet, one only has to visit a few class assignment web sites to realize that, in numerous locations throughout cyberspace, student writers overlook visual rhetoric. Too many Flash, Java, or Shockwave applets, gigantic images, busily colored backgrounds featuring tiny fonts or ill-conceived color combinations between fonts and backgrounds, or incomprehensible objects in MOOs or unintelligible content are just some of the common writing and image errors that occur in e-texts. In many instances, the writers are not thinking about their audience's reception of the e-text. Although the printed content may be the work of a genius and could easily receive an A if the information were in papertext form, if visitors have to wait while four or five applets load (and stall or freeze the reader's machine) or if readers have to squint to read the text because of poor font sizing or mismatched color selections, then the writer's rhetorical decisions are inappropriate. In some instances, if the lack of visual rhetorical knowledge is extreme, visitors may classify the writer as being nonliterate.

So web page design is another transparent act that is in/visible. Speaking as one who worked in graphic design for a few years, I know that what is made visible on the page requires numerous invisible actions, particularly when a writer attempts to coordinate words with images, color, and sound These unseen actions make a huge difference in an e-text's clarity and coherence. It takes practice—sometimes much practice—for students to integrate multimedia sources in some type of proportion to the written content. If writing teachers neglect visual rhetoric and concentrate solely on the written word, then as Takayoshi (1996) suggested, networked writing instruction may become a technological version of current–traditional writing practices as instructors focus on the students' use of form, surface errors, and mechanics.

A second result of the mundane text going online is the appearance of multiple, distinct social positions emerging from the reading of the e-text. We can call this action *perspective*. Perspective is what motivates the establishment of connections, of determining what representations writers and readers want to see each time an e-text is pulled up on screen. This development is especially recognizable when viewing a body of electronic discussion threads from a networked class, whether in e-mail or MOO form. Perspective unfolds as students jump in for one, two, or three sentences, respond with emoticons or capitalized letters to particularly salient or repugnant points made by classmates, create secondary discussions, and use linguistic forms that share qualities from formal written genres (e.g., salutations and closings) as well as informal spoken language (e.g., slang, jargon, or phonemics). If the instructor participates in online discussions, then the students' developing perspective also depends on the instructor's perspective as it relates to the shifting topics.

Over time, such as spanning an entire semester, writing teachers discover the cultural and social patterns and histories that form the teachable—and not so teachable—moments in the classroom. Depending on the instructor's perspective, a teachable or not so teachable moment might be those postings Joan Tornow called "underlife," a term borrowed from sociologist Erving Goffman (Tornow, 1997, pp. 96–106). Underlife postings provide an alternative cultural history for the class. Students tell us more in their emotional reactions and extracurricular discussions of readings, assignments, exchanges with each other, external events, and so on. The study of students' underlife posts could offer another understanding of the syllabus, work load, and community building than the official documents (i.e., filed syllabi, fixed assignment sheets, and student evaluations) suggest. Underlife messages also correspond perfectly to Kress' understanding of the mundane text (1994)—these posts carry the class' pulse and reflect how subcultures within a community of writers respond to the everyday flow of information in the writing course. Therefore, from an assessment perspective, particularly from a programmatic assessment perspective, writing specialists should consider these seemingly trivial messages as part of the research needed to comprehend what exactly happens in the networked writing class.

Although fascinating reading, and often representative of a series of real moments when classroom authority undergoes decentralization, underlife postings can be easily misinterpreted by outsiders as students showing disinterest in the course or the writing process, disrespect to their peers or instructor, or a display of general incivility in their discourse. Also, because of their polyvocality and their context-dependency, these particular discussion threads may seem confusing, vexing, or maundering to the external assessor or to anyone outside of the immediate writing community.

Therefore, in assessment settings, underlife postings can support the opposition's claim of loose grammar instruction or a lack of mechanics being taught in the classroom, because the e-mail subgenre is rooted in vernacular rather than formal or professional language use. Writing instructors who decide to include transcripts of underlife postings in their assessment materials risk the skeptics' or opponents' scorn. Those who doubt the value of internetworked writing in the composition classroom can and will point to these examples as being illustrative of "poor quality control" (read *grade inflation*), "poor academic placement" (read *lower student ability levels for course*), or "weak instructional curricula" (read *promising but misguided idea for the classroom*). One must tread lightly in his or her decision to take heavily context-dependent materials and incorporate them into an assessment portfolio or presentation without the construction of some sort of framing mechanism from which external readers can draw to render judgment. These comments about grade inflation, weak student abilities, and misguided ideas for the classroom point us toward the difficulties some writing instructors have with assessing many e-texts. The boundaries of the students' writing processes are blurred; with techniques like cut and paste or tools like scanners and laser printers and e-mail that make writing in/visible, who knows what is a first draft or a final draft? That is why it becomes so critical to ensure that a student's visual rhetorical ability stands equal to his or her written rhetorical skill. Students must be aware of the many contexts in which their work may be read as well as of the many audiences who may read the work.

However, demanding that students sharpen their visual rhetorical skills may challenge a writing instructor's own control over textual production in networked spaces. The professor may not possess the knowledge or the comfort level to evaluate more than surface errors in the writing. In some instances, the professor may not even know how to use the software a student used to create an internetworked writing form. Or the professor may only have a rudimentary understanding of how something like HTML or even e-mail functions. There also may be instances where the instructor feels that if he or she reduces the emphasis on surface error to focus more on the visual rhetoric, then claims of poor quality control or weak instructional curriculum can sneak more easily into performance reviews or recontracting dossier letters. Last, some faculty members may sense that they must grade surface errors rather than the more complex visual rhetoric issues because they or their writing programs view internetworked writing activities as being akin to journaling.

Still, if instructors are going to assign writing activities in networked spaces, they must find a way to assess those assignments if this work is to be given any serious consideration by students, administrators, or other faculty members. This causes another problem with evaluating mundane e-texts. These e-texts are slippery ones to assess because they conform more to professional writing or everyday writing needs compared with the culturally salient texts or aesthetically valued texts preferred in most academic circles. The two latter groupings illustrate traditional textuality in ways that mundane texts do not. Culturally salient and aesthetically valued texts are rule or convention driven and dependent on extensive top-down or linear beginning-to-end structures to function properly. Conversely, mundane texts link to pragmatic issues for specific outcomes. Moreover, the language use that occurs in mundane texts also echoes informal, pragmatic usage. Additionally, the mundane text category frequently blurs the boundaries of conventional genres—such as when a Ben and Jerry's annual business report chronicles a corporation's cultural or social history or a *Wall Street Journal* or *Los Angeles Times* article draws on the language of academics to discuss an economic or societal problem. This genre boundary blurs even further when a student writing in hypertext links to both or either of these artifacts in her webbed research report as supporting evidence. Consequently, the result of this type of writing is a much different form of literacy and language use than what many composition specialists are used to in that now we have a hybrid genre grounded in traditional information-based forms and more contemporary visual literacy being used in academic settings. Writing that was once salient or belletristic has evolved into communicative acts.

Through technological convergence in Composition, then, writing as a form of communication rather than as an academic activity becomes what Kress called "multisemiotic." In a multisemiotic context, written language combines with visual imagery to transfer information—some information will be better communicated through written language, whereas other information will be best served if exchanged in a visual format (Kress, 1998, pp. 61–65). We can refine our understanding of this transformation by suggesting, pace Kress, "information that *displays* what the world is like is carried by the image; information that orients the reader to that information is carried by language" (1998, p. 65).

All this leads compositionists to revisit our theories and expectations of what writing does, what the text does, and what literacy is in convergence. Until the last decade, college writing generally served the purpose of educating students in the ways of discovering and researching a knowledge base or of pursuing some unattainable truth. Once that information was amassed, students then learned how to pass on the material to as wide and as general (or as discipline specific, depending on the writing class's level) an audience as possible. Texts had fixed meaning because every individual text was another step toward reaching the unobtainable truth. Literacy in this model functions on a deficit approach, because no one discovers sufficient knowledge. Or if someone does present sufficient knowledge, the possibility is great for not having the ability to express it in appropriate ways. As Kathleen Tyner noted, with preconvergence literacy, "the focus is on exploring weaknesses and contradictions in the body of knowledge; students are responsible for making sense of the information; and all students are not expected to do equally well" (1997, p. 46).

Comparably, current writing assessment models also function on a deficit approach to literacy. Whether indirect or direct assessment is used, the philosophy has been to focus on exploring weaknesses and contradictions in what students know about writing. Likewise, in many instances, instructors follow the premise that all students in a class are not expected to do equally well.

Composition's convergence with computers expands the notion of what it means for an individual to write to various social, political, economic, and cultural conditions. Convergence also requires compositionists to reconsider how we assess one's literacy. Thus, through convergence, writing instructors can hold out hope for the act of writing and literacy becoming more inclusive than both may be in present academic settings. Tyner argued, and I agree with her analysis, that convergence shatters the monolithic understanding of literacy into smaller, multiliteracy blocs that correspond to "oral/aural, visual, and alphabetic/text modalities" (1997, p. 60). This multimodality is the characteristic that has the potential to reduce what many writing teachers consider the violence in literacy. Similarly to what postmodern and poststructural theories proposed for truth in the 1960s to 1990s, once literacy diffuses into multiple literacies, no single form of literacy is positioned ahead of another. Each type of literacy can run concurrently with the others. The difficult question becomes, How can we assess these multiple literacies?

Thinking about multiliteracies for Composition acknowledges the various competencies and learning preferences student writers bring with them to the classroom experience that are drawn from race, class, gender, sexual orientation, and physical ability as well as general interest. Teaching writing in the technologically converged classroom, then, means that writing specialists can offer more opportunities for students to become adept in several literacies beyond those they come to class with on the first day. Presently, our society daily handles orality, visuality, and textuality quite well in various media contexts. Melding these aspects into computer-mediated writing experiences should enrich our students' literacy levels while still focusing on the relationship of a writer and a reader to the text.

As Composition moves increasingly toward greater use of networked writing and the formation of networked communities of writers in the classroom, how faculties adjust their definitions of *text* and what their expectations are for an acceptable text in an online environment become critical. A writing teacher's enthusiasm alone for computer-assisted writing instruction and for the use of e-texts that emerge from her students' learning experiences in networked spaces will not be enough to motivate change, however. If the axiom "assessment drives instruction" is to hold any power as convergence continues between computers and writing assessment, then Composition must consider in greater depth what the implications are for assessment should mundane texts persist in internetworked environments.

TRANSFORMING ASSESSMENT

In writing assessment—regardless of whether it takes a holistic, primary trait, scalar, or portfolio form—educators also generally rely on a traditional understanding of transparency to measure the writing and the presence of literacy. That is, the assessors expect to see the text's physical representation to determine how the writer put the finished pieces together in ways recognized by authoritative Others in society. In these situations, narratives and personal experiences take on a particular structure that differs from expository or argument and research writing. Consequently, writing assessment technology maintains strong modernist roots that correspond well to the culturally salient or aesthetically valued texts described earlier in this chapter as compared with the mundane text. These roots evolved from the long history of heuristics, rules, constraints, and perceptions that guide learned writing. By studying the text's form and how well the student writer uses various techniques to create his or her own text, evaluators make inferences about the ways in which a writer constructed the work and what skill level to rank the writer.

Irrespective of the assessment method used, all models are grounded in the behaviorist notion that an instructor can read and assess student writing from repeatedly observing, separating, and classifying student prose into specific categories that connect to the instructor's prior expectations about a writing genre. If writing teachers look carefully at the groupings used to prepare the different checklists or scoring guides implemented in common writing assessment situations, it should be noted that transparency extends only to what the evaluator can actually see—the surface errors and structure. The real inner workings of a student composing an essay, a narrative, a research paper, or a portfolio are obscured. Evaluators cannot peer into the minds of student writers as they compose to see the interconnectivity of thoughts and idea patterns.

Instead, evaluation rubrics are created to assess and measure what is visible in a student's writing. However, these templates are little more than representative criteria for what good writing is in a given context. These rubrics are then applied to a representation of student works to ascertain whether a student reached a prescribed competency level. In some writing situations, as Bob Broad (2002) noted, rubrics are not helpful for teachers making an evaluation. So what we find is that in many assessment contexts, writing specialists use representations to measure representations. We must be aware, though, that some compositionists and certainly educational test and measurement practitioners hold the view that professionally designed assessment tools like rubrics do indeed measure what is intended to be measured and that these mechanisms offer students and instructors closure. Yet, as I point out in chapter 4, there is far more to this discussion than surface or predictive validity when handling electronic texts. Compositionists as well as test and measurement specialists must find a new language to describe how validity and reliability functions with electronic writing.

Although conventional writing assessment provides closure to a writing class, a composition sequence, or a graduating student's academic career, it may be more opaque than transparent for what really happens in a student's composing processes, particularly in online classes. For those who teach some or all of their writing classes in a networked environment, the opacity of traditional writing assessment for measuring students' online thinking and writing becomes all too apparent. To accommodate the changes in thinking, organizing, and developing behaviors that a student writer undergoes in an internetworked writing space, writing assessment must also be transformed to reflect the types of skills, essential writer's knowledge, and discursive strategies needed to be literate in a technological environment.

Computers certainly make postmodern considerations of language and thought transparent in the visible sense. We can see the fragmentation of syntax, the brevity of response (thought), and the collapse of traditional papertext boundaries in any number of electronic publications. This transformation occurs particularly in hypertexts, which, as Johndan Johnson-Eilola noted, make "visible the operations and effects of powerful modern theories of reading and writing—postmodernism and poststructuralism, reader-response criticism and critical literacy, and collaborative learning and social construction theory" (in Selfe & Hilligoss, 1994, p. 196). Consequently, the change is a problem for current notions of writing assessment—including portfolio assessment—because what grounds much of assessment theory is drawn from either what Brian Huot called "a Platonic universe and positivist epistemology ... an idealized universal truth that assumes a single correct answer" or "an assumption that professional editors or teachers are qualified to make [assessment] decisions based upon their experience and expertise" (1998, p. 103, brackets mine). If writing teachers follow the Platonic ideal, and a good number still do, then much of networked writing must certainly appear incoherent.

Likewise, if compositionists evaluate e-texts based on a situation and appraise each student's e-text without some criteria, along the lines of Jean-François Lyotard's concept of judging without criteria, then assessment drifts into a subjective space that can be hard for some instructors to defend. After all, in postmodernism as in Internet discourse, who can claim that one's experience or expertise is more valid and valued than another's? To suggest in networked writing that the teacher's experiences or expertise is more validated than the student writers' is slippery, because many students now come to technology-infused composition classes with far more expertise and experience in computer literacy than a number of their instructors.

What may even be worse for assessment in this circumstance is that writing instructors enter computer-based writing classrooms without much expertise in the various language and graphics tools used to construct e-texts. They may also have little background in postmodern theories of texts and language that address fragmentary syntax and discourse. There may also be a lack of understanding of the postprocess approach to composition, in which writing is situated for public view beyond the classroom. Yet these writing teachers are expected to evaluate writing that is highly associative and connective rather than linear, writing that is often without closure when compared with the more familiar papertexts that respond nicely to modernist evaluation techniques. This problem creates an even wider gap in teacher-generated evaluation of e-texts, because greater numbers of students now move about comfortably in networked environments because their earlier schooling or home experiences are increasingly linked to computers. In the very near future, a significant amount of students may have more authority in working with e-texts than many of their professors. Compositionists should surely expect this trend toward hyperliterate computer users entering their classes to continue in the future, because state legislatures, public and private K–12 schools, and parents have made teaching with technology a primary goal for elementary and secondary education in the 21st century. Until Composition's culture as a whole recognizes the necessity for its practitioners to have more than a basic understanding of how to teach writing using computers and until composition and rhetoric programs implement a series of courses for graduate students and current writing faculty to show them how to incorporate these two technologies, it will be difficult to promote the development of reasonable, pedagogically sound measurement practices for networked writing beyond what currently exists. While the field awaits the occurrence of these events, it opens itself to external charges of a lack in accountablity that may not be true but still cannot be defended because little has been articulated.

For the sake of argument, let us say that Composition's convergence between computer technology and writing assessment can usher in a more humane, more performative, student-centered type of evaluation process than has existed to date. The push for electronic portfolio grading, most recently discussed by Trent Batson (2002) and the NCTE statement on writing assessment (2001), reflects this growing trend toward greater student autonomy in writing assessment. Brian Huot's most recent work (2002) proposed that it is time for Composition to (re)articulate writing assessment, and I concur. Not only do compositionists need to learn how to read and respond differently, as Huot elegantly argued, but writing specialists have to think differently about what a text is in the writing classroom and how a text functions in cyberspace. This means instructors have to become more comfortable with the place of the mundane text in the teaching of writing.

As Composition makes the turn toward introducing mundane texts in writing classes, even at the first-year levels, the field will eventually see writing that is less academic and more performative in public spaces. A synergy between visual and textual rhetoric must also emerge over time to motivate a change in the presentation of what writing is in this environment and how students' multiple literacies become engaged in the writing process. Mundane texts can help students and instructors understand this interconnectedness between visual and textual rhetoric because those texts speak to wider audiences and demand that writers and readers use a range of literacies to comprehend the information contained within them.

As students become comfortable with using both mundane texts and multiple literacies in networked environments, compositionists can also count on students becoming even more aware of how texts are read by others. A result of this evolution in evaluation becomes real student ownership of the text. Student writers truly come to accept responsibility for putting colored marks on a blank screen and do not merely replicate what they see their instructors modeling for them in the front of the room. At last, Composition's culture becomes genuinely democratic and progressive. Students and their instructors together share power with words instead of one having power over another's words. Assessment becomes an extension of dialogue among authors in a writing community instead of an adversarial experience.

Is this possible? Is this Utopic thinking?

Perhaps. Then again, perhaps not.

What will make this proposed situation a reality in Composition's culture is a radical reconception of what assessment is for the e-text. Writing assessment needs to address the diversity found in e-texts and the diversity of the electronic writing process. The type of writing assessment that composition studies should call for in an age of technological convergence corresponds to the following six points:

- Acknowledges the complexities of the communication environment, the online writing process, and the technologies involved in producing an interactive environment
- Perceives students who write in networked spaces to be published authors and grants those students the same rights and privileges as other writers in a scholarly environment
- Recognizes and articulates the multiple forms of information needed across diverse communication situations
- Considers the students' ability to select applicable tools or sources that conform to the discourse community (or communities) that students occupy
- Confirms students' capability to evaluate textual materials across multiple mediums and formats
- Demonstrates students' awareness of and aptitude for manipulating and organizing acquired information across multiple media, formats, and computer operating system platforms

- Shows that students are acquainted with and can perform specific technological applications and processes to transmit information to a variety of familiar and unfamiliar online audiences (adapted from Dupuis, 1997)

Readers should notice that the words *competence, skill, product,* and other like terms reflective of earlier assessment procedures are absent from this model. In place of these older notions, a greater emphasis is placed on communication and community, interactive and multiple discourse situations and formats, and the process of writing in and for networked contexts.

This is an important shift in how compositionists define writing assessment for two central reasons. First, instead of approaching the act of assessing writing as being primarily an exploration into the deficiencies in student writing, this reconfigured assessment philosophy accounts for writers' assets and what knowledge students acquire over a term. The outcomes in a rubric are asking writing teachers not just to measure skill development but also to consider the students' range of awareness about the roles of various technological resources and options and how those might function to resolve a writer's problems when composing for a networked audience. Second, radicalizing the language of assessment by eliminating traditional terminology asks writing instructors to reconceptualize evaluation instruments as being a creative force instead of a norming force. The significance of this second point should not go unnoticed in many higher educational settings, where our diverse student populations lean toward literacies that are undervalued by standard norming assessment procedures. This trend will continue to occur in the years ahead as more students from wider social and racial spectra enter American colleges and universities. Instead of reinforcing the "right" way of thinking about online writing to students (whatever criteria the right way may follow), the emphasis in evaluation becomes less a matter of correctness and more a dialogue between students and instructors about the text based on applicable evidence that emerges from the e-text.

An assessment philosophy for networked writing like the one proposed here works with students' multiple literacies without punishing students for being less inclined to favor an institutionally dominant literacy. So students who are strongly visually literate or aurally literate and who are weaker in alphabetic literacy can discover innovative ways to write and communicate that incorporate their strengths through the inclusion of graphics or sound as well as through some placement of conventional alphabetic text. Also, this assessment model accounts for the variety of e-texts students can produce now and into the future as technology changes. Whether individually or in collaboration with their peers, this concept accounts for shifts in modalities. Last, this proposed set of assessment outcomes respects students as real writers with genuine audiences instead of seeing students as writer-apprentices who are learning their lines.

Skeptical readers might be wondering how writing teachers can implement such an assessment proposal into the networked composition class. Although this point is addressed more fully in later chapters, suffice it to say here that much of the assessment can be accomplished using some of the basic, recognized methods compositionists now rely on to conduct peer group evaluations—checklists, portfolio responses, and student self-assessment activities, as well as protocol interviews. However, the manner in which writing specialists apply these items needs to be revisited and reclaimed. Instead of studying the students' texts upon completion, instructors appraise stages of the students' electronic writing to reflect more authentic assessment.

Over time, as technology and new ideas regarding how to evaluate e-texts develop, these methods will need to be refined and expanded to adapt to the newer forms. Unlike writing assessment since the 1870s, the practices instructors use to evaluate e-texts will have to be revised regularly to keep pace with rapid technological change. As Trent Batson's (2002) article in *Syllabus* magazine indicated, e-portfolios are emerging across college and university campuses as the next new technological thing in assessment. As Batson described his University of Rhode Island e-portfolio experience, the model merely ports over traditional papertext concepts and places them into an electronic format. Composition has taken one older form of technology (the portfolio, which has a 25-year history) and transported it to a newer form (the Internet). Although e-portfolios may work now in the early 21st century, as instructors and programs are in the dawning stages of merging these two technologies, it is entirely conceivable that computer technology will transform itself many times over in the next few decades. These transformations will also alter how we write and how we think of texts. Therefore, in their current state, e-portfolios cannot remain a single answer for evaluating networked writing. As computing changes, so too must assessment. This point will be taken up in greater detail in chapters 4 and 5.

MESHING LEARNING OUTCOMES WITH TRANSFORMED ASSESSMENT PRACTICES

At many colleges and universities, the talk about instruction now centers on "learning outcomes"; that is, what do professors or departments expect their students to know upon finishing a class or a course of study? Starting with this point as the base for a revised approach to writing assessment for online assignments, here are four broadly conceived criteria that reflect the dominant composition and rhetorical practices found in most writing programs and that adapt to electronic communication but fit with the proposed assessment model:

- Students demonstrate a critical analysis of how networked writing is constructed and is received by audiences in various historical, social, and cultural contexts.
- Students exhibit that online writing is a constructive process that depends upon a writer making certain choices and selections or changing specific elements of the text or image to control the message sent to the reader.
- Students rely on multiple forms or genres in electronic communication to produce a range of teacher-assigned and self-selected projects.
- Students develop the rhetorical and technological techniques and skills necessary to write and communicate in a networked environment.

These four criteria can be modified to fit most writing programs' needs, as the best writing assessment tends to be localized to the demands of each institution. For those who may be unclear as to how to establish individualized criteria for their programs, I offer a heuristic based on my undergraduate and graduate courses.

First, students demonstrate a critical analysis of how networked writing is constructed and is received by audiences in various historical, social, and cultural contexts. The following individual criteria are used to measure this goal (assignments in this section are completed either online or in papertext form):

1. Students examine a social problem in real life that has similar effects in virtual communities (i.e., illiteracy, addiction, rape, freedom of religion, privacy rights, hate speech, racism, sexual discrimination).
2. Students investigate many web sites, electronic discussion lists, Usenet groups, chat rooms, or MOOs to evaluate the ways language, image, sound, and color affect homogenous and heterogenous audiences based on race, class, gender, political affiliation, physical ability, geographic region, or age.
3. Students participate in various electronic discussion formats outside of the classroom experience to discern how well the written text substitutes for spoken language and how audiences (mis)interpret concrete and abstract words in the textual messages they receive.

Second, students exhibit that online writing is a constructive process that depends on a writer making certain choices and selections or changing specific elements of the text or image to control the message sent to the reader. The following individual criteria are used to measure this goal:

1. Students create their own discourse rules to maintain and moderate their class discussion list.
2. Students create external discussion lists or blogs using freeware on a topic of interest and solicit members to join and stay with the list or blog. Students choose to create moderated or unmoderated lists and must select avenues for broadcasting the existence of their lists or blogs.
3. Students write in various mediums (hypertext and HTML, specifically) and incorporate graphics, sound, and motion in their nonfiction and fiction writing to test the effectiveness of incorporating different media elements in an e-text and to discover which media each student prefers for writing. Also, students discover that some genres react differently to a change in technological medium, which causes multiple reactions in an audience.

Third, students rely on multiple forms or genres of electronic communication to produce a range of teacher-assigned and self-selected projects. The following individual criteria are used to measure this goal:

1. Students complete a series of short, teacher-directed assignments to acquire the basic techniques and skills needed to do a larger project in a particular medium.
2. Students develop a base repertoire of networked writing strategies from which to develop longer, more complex collaborative or individual projects.
3. Students design and create an end-of-term project of their own choosing that incorporates two or three of the electronic forms discussed (i.e., a web page linking viewers to an original listserv and blog or a hypertext chapbook of poetry and a companion web site). This may or may not be a webfolio of work.

Fourth, students develop the rhetorical and technological techniques and skills necessary to write and communicate in a networked environment. The following individual criteria are used to measure this goal:

1. Students know and use the terms of technological production and can discuss the rhetorical effects these terms elicit in an audience.
2. Students cast a critical eye at the electronic and paper texts they consume and question both media's effects on the viewer or reader.
3. Students judge a web site, a discussion list, a hypertext composition, a MOO, or a weblog by studying its effects on the intended viewer, what issues the e-text raises for the writer and the audience, and the potential power the e-text has for enacting change or action in the audience.

Some may ask where the emphasis is on grammar, mechanics, and structure, the trinity found in most assessment rubrics. Let me suggest here that technological convergence challenges older, more prescriptive notions of what entails "good writing," "good grammar," "proper mechanics," and "fine structure" in communicating with others. This is a point many instructors discover when they read postings on Usenet, chat, or discussion lists. People tend to understand the faux pas of typing too fast, relying on acronyms, or using the inventive syntax that sometimes occurs when writers are trying to capture content. We accept these "errors" when corresponding with peers but not with students. Far too often the hallmarks of good writing regarding computers and writing focus on the word-processing abilities of a student writer. However, writing instructors must take care not to equate interactive writing with word processing; the two are very different methods for composing and each rely on particular ways for students to classify the written word. Therefore, let me offer a brief description of what good writing often means in networked environments.

In interactive writing contexts, for instance, good writing tends to mean layering the e-text with multiple sensory and support experiences. That is why e-texts include many elements from hyperlinks to archived data, to PowerPoint slide shows and Quick Time movies, to a link to a discussion site, to gallery exhibits of still photos, to any number of other possibilities that regularly emphasize a personal voice over an instructive one. Generally, networked writers' personalized discursive structures attempt to foster audience interaction with the text, to establish what Ann Hill Duin and Craig Hansen described as "situational literacy" (in Selfe & Hilligoss, 1994, p. 98). According to Duin and Hansen (1994), situational literacy resists external pressures from those outside the immediate community of writers. So, not only do student writers have to master multiple literacies in the production of an e-text, but they must also learn how to negotiate situational literacy. Therefore, when student writers' immediate electronic community reflects a nonacademic culture, the writer will adopt a less academic discourse style (perhaps even adopting an alternative discourse style). This is what writing teachers often see in underlife postings to a class list, for instance. The students are not seeing the class list discussion as part of the academic culture and take up nonacademic speech styles and subjects. Clearly this reflects the students' misreading of the situation.

Conversely, in situational literacy, if students are part of a writing community that is more academic or professional in character, they will write in a corresponding manner. This frequently happens when students directly respond to a text in an online assignment or when they are engaged in e-mail exchanges with a member of the professional community a student aspires to enter (Duin & Hansen, 1994). In these networked writing spaces, as Denise Murray noted, student writers adapt "their composing processes to the particular task environment, [and] create a new mode of discourse, one that is more appropriate for particular tasks…, for particular interpersonal relations…, and for particular modes" (1991, p. 53). In short, situational literacy coincides with the multimodal representations found in electronic communication and depends on students' understanding of multiple literacies to correctly decipher the context.

Some may argue that students in traditional classroom settings also adopt these multiliteracy roles to write their assignments. My response to this is that in internetworked writing spaces, students are not adopting the roles; instead of posing as the student who would contact Biologist Z or Journalist Y, students writing online are contacting biologists, journalists, and so on. To successfully communicate with various professionals, students need to learn the language, the rhetorical and discursive styles, and the basic knowledge necessary to hold conversations with those already in a specialty. In these electronic exchanges with professionals, students must discover how to become situationally literate and adapt to the multimodal conditions that exist in internetworked writing experiences.

Thinking about using computers to teach writing in this way is completely different from thinking about using computers to show students how to word process documents or to import graphics into a text. Word processing can easily correspond with more current–traditional understandings of textual production and its emphasis on student writers producing a "correct" document compared with writing with HTML, SGML, ASP, or Perl scripts. The word-processing approach is also more subject to instructor dominance over the text because there is a very curbed interchange of ideas and information between student writer and master teacher. The resulting papertext conforms to familiar textual structures in ways that e-texts do not. As such, an instructor's use of the word-processing approach makes it much easier for him or her to impose more intrusive assessment on student work. This can occur because the instructor knows how a course paper should look; no one knows what an e-text should look like—not even the most experienced writing instructor.

It is this not knowing what an e-text officially looks like or should have as its purpose that makes evaluating one so difficult. Who can say what the subject matter's purpose is for an e-text? To impart information, yes, but surely there is more than that at work in most e-texts. One could argue that writers of electronic texts need to know who their potential readers are and what their expectations and beliefs are. This idea works well for classroom assignments with a fixed audience, but the potential readership on the

World Wide Web is, well, worldwide—who can account for all the cultural and educational expectations and beliefs a global readership has? Certainly only a very few spectacular writers of the last millennium have had this ability. The purpose of an e-text can be so many things depending on who accesses the text and when the accessing occurs. At best, the student writer can perhaps identify the primary and secondary audiences her web site or postings may address; in some instances, a student writer may be able to provide a tertiary audience for the work. Perhaps as students' access to and ability with e-texts grow in the years ahead, we can expect and demand more from them with regard to outlining a global audience. For now, unless the writing is produced in a limited environment, like a closed BBS (Bulletin Board System) or restricted listserv, expecting students to have a complete grasp of the discourse structure needed to produce a successful web site, weblog, or MOO may be difficult. This is because online class assignments really cease to be "class assignments" once students leave the course or post them to the web. In cyberspace, these earlier assignments become an artifact, a bit of information webbed with other bits, a declaration of some knowledge put forward by a writer who has moved on.

All this suggests that in networked space, student writers are not apprentices: They are writers and authors. Equally, in networked space, instructors are not masters: They too are writers and authors. Thus, from a networked space a community of writers emerges. In such a community, how one shares authority and power as well as how one discusses her progress reflects the levels of ownership one believes she has. Currently, in many composition classes—even the computer-based classes—an imbalance exists in how authority, power, and ownership are configured in assessment. This is so even with the more egalitarian e-portfolio. Although students submit their best work, often with some type of reflective element to the portfolio, the true evaluation comes from the instructor and not some external audience that responds to the students' texts.

As technical convergence transforms the present state of the text in Composition, it must also lead to transforming assessment as well. In the future, authentic assessment in classes that use networked writing may require writing instructors to relinquish some of their control, their power over the text, to others who are outside the classroom and who wish to comment and critique the student writers' efforts. Encouraging outsiders to read, review, and comment on class hypertexts, MOOs, blogs, web pages, and so on makes evaluation more real, more legitimate, for writers. This approach treats student writers as the authors they are. Students then must own their words and the content of their pages, blogs, and the like, as all writers must do at some point.

However, with electronic communication, a student's words have a greater potential for impact than if the words were placed in a papertext assignment or portfolio. The external critiques, then, demonstrate how well a student has captured the concept of situational literacy. These outside responses also show to what extent a student has honed her multiple literacies as a technorhetor.

To help readers who are unfamiliar with how an external evaluation might benefit students in networked classes, let me draw on a familiar situation in the traditional classroom format. If, for instance, a student fails to communicate her point about the physical effects of natural-based steroids to an interested web surfer who happened to log on to her page for more information, is what transpired more serious than scoring a 2 or a 3 on an end-of-term holistic essay? Some instructors might argue that the student who has miscommunicated information through her web page has committed a more egregious error than scoring poorly on a one-shot essay. The incorrect or obtuse data the surfer may obtain during his visit could cause physical harm or great confusion; remember, for some people, a *.edu* site suggests that all the information is carefully vetted—even though the link may be clearly labeled as containing classroom research. That is why visitors who log onto students' web pages or other e-texts should be asked to evaluate the work for content and readability (perhaps even navigablity and usability as students become more facile with technology). Visitors always have the option of not doing an evaluation; however, a number of them will respond, and students then receive genuine evaluative feedback on their writing from someone who has no connection to the outcome of the class but who has a strong interest in the topic. Students can then measure these responses in relation to the instructor's or their peers' comments.

Rather than risk the flames of passing along erroneous or embarrassing information to the world, most students will revise ill-conceived or poorly constructed passages if someone in cyberspace points them out. Over time and with comments flowing from the teacher, one's peers, and the external audience, authentic revision occurs and students begin to understand what it means to be a writer who has real ownership of the words she writes. Authentic assessment occurs without the instructor having sole power over the student.

Is it possible or even desirable for instructors to create a community of writers with their students when assessment is involved? In an era of technological convergence, it may be the only way to keep a human presence connected to either computer use or assessment procedures. Although a computer-based classroom does not in itself ensure a constructivist classroom, it does enable one happening. Likewise, forms of writing assessment such as the e-portfolio or external review of student webbed writing do not guarantee constructivist assessment; they do encourage the possibility of it occurring. In the constructivist voice of either computer-assisted instruction or writing assessment, the human presence is retained to give polish and refinement to the messages and texts that writers develop across time and space. Together in convergence, the two strands of technology blend with constructivist thinking and can lead to the following six points so critical for students' progress in writing:

- Students will come to know the uses and limitations of computer technology, texts produced through the use of computer technology, and the range of discursive strategies needed to communicate with others.
- Students will come to know both a depth and a breadth of knowledge that arise from researching a topic and writing about it through hyperlinking. The depth emerges from the process of inquiry; the breadth arises from the surface presence of links to multiple URL sites.
- Students will come to know the criteria others use to judge the quality of an electronic text, how an electronic text should be judged within various contexts, and how to secure evidence to measure a text's value according to different audiences' contexts and criteria.
- Students will come to know how to create an effective electronic text and how to write to accommodate a global or a local audience.
- Students will come to know how to select information appropriate for their electronic texts that will be useful for a particular situation but could be understood by a wide audience.

- Students will come to know how to evaluate an electronic text effectively, fairly, and efficiently through their interactions with other writers and thinkers (adapted from Hopkins, 1998).

So, yes, it is possible and desirable for compositionists and their programs to develop a community of writers to address writing assessment in an age of technological convergence. Not only will this action encourage keeping a human's touch on two potentially distancing technologies, a point that is often raised to counter the use of computers in the writing classroom, but it will also open student writers to multiple, public audiences who can engage students with new views and opportunities for reader response. The result of this community building can be an assessment mechanism that is both truly authentic and can address the problem of the mundane text in the writing class.

In the electronic transformation of what compositionists know as *the text*, the door is left open to transform what the culture of Composition knows as writing assessment. Many mundane e-texts conform to the ludic facets of postmodernism as they transcend historical time and space, draw on free-floating signifiers, and shatter the production of linear connections. Yet mundane e-texts can also maintain a resistant strain of postmodernism in that they break apart the traditional power structures and reconfigure power, knowledge, and motives more evenhandedly compared with the traditional texts that instructors study during their graduate and post graduate years. As writing programs are pressured to include more internetworked writing assignments and more faculty discover the divergent qualities of paper and pixelized texts, the e-texts' failure to submit to traditional writing assessment practices will cause compositionists to question the time-honored understandings of assessment. It is this latter tension that e-texts place on writing assessment that Composition and compositionists must focus on as electronic literacy becomes more pervasive in society. This tension that the e-text puts on assessment will lead us to newer, fairer, more authentic ways to evaluate our students' writing.

Chapter 3

Who Owns
the Words in Electronic Texts?

New media technology changes so quickly—and all too often, both culturally and economically, colleges and faculty lag behind. Even if writing instructors were raised in the television or video culture, making the leap to multimedia communication is sometimes difficult. The cognitive processes needed to encode and decode the layers of messaging at times border on information overload for compositionists who are tied closely to the printed page. The cultural and economic lag also extends to institutions facing the constant hardware and software upgrades needed to keep pace with the advances in a computer's internal architecture. Without continual proper training of faculty and regular upgrades and maintenance of machines, a computer-based writing environment quickly can be rendered obsolete.

Yet our classrooms are filled with students who move easily though web pages and weblogs filled with Shockwave or MP3 audio, Quick Time video, hyperlinks, and Flash applets. Students are comfortable adapting to the cutting edge of technological advances because they are steeped in this culture. From cell phones to pagers to laptop computers with DVD burners and portable DVD players, most of our students have a technological awareness that stretches to their language use as well. They not only want to read information in this newer technological manner, but they also want to write and produce information the same way.

Literacy for these students is not confined to traditional alphabetic or belletristic forms. Students increasingly realize that literacy is now a convergence of information from a variety of sources, both print and electronic. The acronym YOYOW (You Own Your Own Words) rings true for many students' communication. And the power inherent in owning one's words—especially in a multimedia world—now extends to the way one writes in a classroom setting.

Carla Hesse, writing in *The Future of the Book* (Nunberg, 1996), suggested that

> the critical distinction between "the book" and other forms of printed matter is not the physical form of the printed word, or the implicit set of social actors that it requires …, but rather the *mode of temporality* that the book form establishes between those actors. The book is a slow form of exchange. It is a mode of temporality which conceives of public communication not as action, but rather as reflection upon action. Indeed the book form serves precisely to defer action, to widen the temporal gap between thought and deed, to create a space for reflection and debate. (p. 27)

Hesse's point is critical for writing teachers, because much of traditional writing depends on the "bookish" sense of temporality and the position that good writing takes time and reflection. Most compositionists hope students create spaces for reflection and debate in their writing, not to act on words hastily but to think and deliberate the ideas that words elicit.

However, this bookish sense of temporality privileged in writing instruction is at odds with the immediacy of electronic communication. E-mail, chat, MOOs, weblogs, and the like are not always reflective genres. These genres beg a call to action from an audience. These mundane texts are public communication in action, and the type of writing involved in producing such e-texts is intended to be both sudden and widespread. E-texts are meant to be interactive, not necessarily reflective. Therefore, these texts provide the writer with great power to inspire an immediate effect on the audience, whether for good or ill.

This shift in the mode of temporality for a writer, from reflective to interactive, changes the role of the student writer in the college composition classroom. Interactive writing parallels oratory, in that writing becomes performative. As with other performative speech acts, the student writer depends on locutionary, illocutionary, and perlocutionary language acts (see Austin, 1962, for a complete discussion of performative speech acts). Locutionary language acts in cyberspace function similarly to other speech contexts—the writer or speaker makes statements regardless of their veracity. Likewise, illocutionary acts demonstrate the force of an action or stating a claim—such as a student on a discussion list ordering another participant to do something or pronouncing another's claim as factual or not. Perlocutionary acts in e-texts achieve certain semantic effects by writing something, for instance, annoying someone through an e-mail flame or by sending a "ditto" post to agree with a point.

Yet cyberwriting is not as simple as Austin (1962) offered. Unlike Austin's rigid distinctions among these three speech act categories, composing in electronic space reinforces Derrida's claim of iterability in writing (1988). In e-texts, the same expressions or word types can occur in different contexts that transform the intended meaning to the degree that multiple, unintended meanings arise beyond the simple speech act categories Austin presents. These iterations give rise to polysemy in e-texts. Moreover, the iterability of speech acts in e-texts suggests that although the student writers have power and intent over their words as they type them on screen, once those words are transmitted into cyberspace, readers can discard the writers' power and intent as being irrelevant. The writers' power and intent become inconsequential as time, place, and conditions under which the audience receives the message shape the speech act. So even though the act of writing on screen frees student writers from the ponderous nature of traditional academic styles of writing in favor of immediacy and interactivity, networked writing demands that students be even more vigilant about the words they select and the rhetorical strategies they use. Frequently, students' words often take on a life of their own when set into cyberspace.

There is no doubt that writing in electronic spaces does indeed infuse writers with power over the words they write. Paul Gilster (1997) noted that the basic distinction between traditional media and the Internet is that instead of offering content, as is the case with traditional media, the individual using the Internet must create the content from the volume of information available to a writer. In a very real sense, student writers do own their own words, as they compile and create new knowledge from found knowledge. With this newfound ownership regarding students' use of language, however, comes not only various levels of rhetorical responsibility but also several concerns related to the production of a student's e-text.

Over the last few years, writing faculty have become particularly sensitive to the kinds of ownership issues that arise when student writers create texts, especially the potential for plagiarism. There are other issues, too, such as intellectual property concerns, collaboration decisions, and right of use. These ownership issues only intensify when a student enters networked writing spaces. Compositionists should realize that the Internet is a public venue made for direct publication of e-texts, analogous to a vanity press; once uploaded, a student writer's web site or course paper can be viewed (and downloaded) by an infinite number of interested readers unless some password-protection system is implemented. Inappropriate sharing of material—from downloading an entire paper to copying and pasting a jpeg image onto a web site—is merely a point and click act. Whereas some appropriations are clearly considered wrong, such as the direct downloading of another's paper, other "borrowings" are not as vilified. Photos, lyrics, music, backgrounds, and the like are often used in building student web sites, but these items are not attributed to the developer nor are copyrights secured. Many times, the common student—and sometimes faculty—(mis)perception is that no one really owns the words, images, or sounds in internetworked spaces. Therefore, appropriation as a way of building resources is acceptable. This notion arises sometimes from what Geoffrey Nunberg described as the "personalism" of the Internet as opposed to the distancing mechanisms of traditional media, including books:

> People speak, not as authors to an anonymous public, but rather in the form of a colloquial conversation between participants who are copresent in the act of speaking. Contributors often address one another directly, where antagonists always refer to each other in the third person. And the style of argument [or the Internet] admits the personal, the anecdotal, the subjective. If you are willing to make allowances (rather a lot of them), the tone recalls the early eighteenth-century periodicals and the first stirrings of the modern critical spirit. (Nunberg, 1996, p. 32, brackets mine)

What Nunberg spoke of runs counter to the mores of contemporary North American academic and professional culture, which is generally antagonistic in its argument structure and depends on citation as acknowledgment of others' ideas. What one may consider "personalism" in a classroom context, however, could bring forth trouble as plagiarism.

Lately, more of these academic perceptions of the Internet's personalism are being challenged legally, as "fair use" for educational purposes concerning cybermaterial drawn from online newspaper and magazine web sites is more strictly defined. Fair use issues and the Internet also extend to online class lectures that are derived extensively from another author's work—these lectures, unless password protected, are subject to "cease and desist" letters or threats of lawsuit (L. Marcus, personal communication, July 1996; Tyner, 1997, p. 84). Students too are prepared to challenge in the courts an instructor's right to the fair use of a student's work for a class with online components. A 1998 suit involving the University of Nebraska–Lincoln and a former UNL student showed that students can file suit against instructors who place their work online without express permission. As a story in the *Chronicle of Higher Education* reported, a student who believes copyright is violated by uploading his or her work may bring legal charges against the professor and the institution ("Former U of Nebraska Student," 1998, A29).

This question of authority is central to both computer-enhanced composition and writing assessment. In each instance, authority is configured much differently. Internetworked writing environments yield full authority to students—including the right not to have their work displayed for public view or the right to password protect their sites from unwanted entry. Following current understandings of intellectual property rights, even in networked classrooms students have the right—and the means—to deny public access to their work. After all, having worldwide access to a student's paper—whether flawed or perfect—is not quite the same as having a transparency of the paper on an overhead in a F2F class setting for a limited number of students to see. Teachers who view student resistance to uploading their papers onto the Internet as trivial should think about the notion of "author's reprint rights," because internetworked writing does carry copyright.

This type of student resistance can be problematic to the point of lawsuit for those instructors who upload student assignments for discussion or evaluation without first seeking their students' permission ("Former U of Nebraska Student," 1998). The democratizing effect of computer-enhanced composition that gives students greater control over their writing can also frustrate many aspects of typical writing assessment practices. In these instances, alternative assessment possibilities must be in place. One such possibility might be for instructors to section off some private space in an online class-room—perhaps a folder or location within the virtual class—that is password protected and only the faculty member and those students who wish to keep their work separate have access to the space. A second prospective idea could be to have these students upload their work directly to the instructor's private working space on the campus network for evaluation (this is only workable for institutions that provide faculty with their own area on the campus system). Another viable method is to separate assignments into uploadable and nonuploadable categories, with the explicit understanding that uploadable assignments are for public display and response. Other workable solutions exist, depending on the local conditions at the college or university, and composition specialists need to plan ahead for students who may wish to exert their control over the work they produce in an internetworked writing class.

Students who actively pursue their authority and their intellectual property rights have never been a concern in more traditional assessment settings. Historically, writing assessment impedes student agency—although, in more recent movements, like the portfolio system, evaluation now grants more student agency than in the past. Yet even this move toward more student-centered assessment in the portfolio does not accommodate resistant students who refuse to provide their instructors with a final portfolio or who offer up an incomplete portfolio. In standard writing assessment procedures, a student's lack of a final portfolio to grade or submission of an incomplete portfolio is treated usually as a failing contribution. To pass a class or to fulfill barrier requirements, students are expected to complete the final assessment procedure in a multiple-choice, essay, or portfolio form. Intellectual property concerns are not an issue here, nor is student authority over the writing. Students are expected to do what they are told regarding assessment or face the consequences. If a student does not want completed electronic assignments made public and no other outlet is made available for review other than web publication, what then? Does the student fail? Receive a grade drop? To date, with the University of Nebraska–Lincoln case, the courts have sided with the student's right to privacy in resisting publication of her work on the Internet, even for class critique. Therefore, options for assessing internetworked writing assignments need to be in place to avoid potential problems.

These ownership issues have profound implications not only for how writing instructors present material but for how they discuss and assess the e-texts that students produce for a class. Just who owns the words written in an e-text produced for a college writing course—the student or the writing instructor? One reaction says, "Well, of course, the students do!" Staunchly pro-assessment folks might counter with whether student ownership of the text is a concern in assessment. It is a concern, particularly in light of the growing legal support for the author's rights in cyberspace. Yet, it is understandable how the pro-assessment reaction stems from the ways in which composition studies have traditionally defined assessment, as evaluating a student's writing an object of study as the culminating educational experience and not as a genuine document.

This position must change in light of Composition's move toward internetworked writing in the classroom. Textual ownership issues in cyberspace are messy and complex. Adding the component of the university and its equipment to the mix further muddies the ownership discussion. Patel (1996) stated that if, for instance, students are using campus networks to do their class web work or list postings, they are exempted from claiming intellectual property privileges on their work. The legal argument here is based on the point that students are not employees of the college or university and so are not afforded the same rights as faculty members who are expected to publish or develop creative work (Patel, 1996). According to Patel's 1996 article in the *Indiana Law Journal*, it is regularly thought that a student whose work is developed under university auspices "should be viewed as part of the educational experience because that work is typically conducted in pursuit of degree certification requirements" (p. 503). Following that interpretation, the pro-assessment position makes sense: Openly assessing a student's work in an online class should be considered part of the educational experience, particularly if the class is part of the degree requirements for graduation. However, under general patent, copyright, and contract law, students have greater intellectual property rights than Patel (1996) suggested they do given their current university status (Newell, 1986; Schlacter, 1997). This is especially true if students complete their assignments using web hosting sites like Geocities or Angelfire, public domain sites not affiliated with universities, and if students depend on a non-university-based internet service provider (ISP) to access these sites. In these situations, Schlacter (1993) wrote, all intellectual property rights do revert to the student, who can then challenge a professor's right to evaluate this work, even if it is produced for a class.

The problem of assessing students' online work becomes equally complicated if the writing classes use university equipment to complete assignments. There is no guarantee the courts will side with the college to allow students' work to be viewed and evaluated via the Internet if a student wishes not to be included in the assessment activities, as the University of Nebraska case illustrates ("Former U of Nebraska Student," 1998). Moreover, there is no assurance the university administration will support a writing instructor's practices for evaluating student work produced online. In the University of Nebraska case, the vice president and counsel for the institution would not defend the English professor in question because it was the university's position that UNL "considers creating the web pages in question to have been outside the professor's responsibilities as a faculty member" (p. A29).

Writing instructors must become far more aware of how intellectual property and copyright laws connect to their students' online work, because ownership issues can have a profound affect on writing assessment in the digital age. Although there appear to be no current suits against colleges or universities with regard to the online use of student texts, the situation could indeed arise again. Assessing students' internetworked writing may become increasingly dependent on legal decisions that are subject to multiple interpretations of contemporary patent, copyright, and contract law—especially if the assessments are connected to some type of benchmark or barrier exam or if a grade is issued based on the evaluation. Therefore, programs considering adopting an information literacy component or an online writing requirement should be in close consultation with the institution's legal counsel to ensure that students, faculty, and programs are protected and their rights are represented.

Assessment is not testing nor is it grading, many composition scholars argue (Blair and Takayoshi, 1997; Huot, 2002; White, 1994; Zak and Weaver, 1998). Assessment is merely challenging both the students' learning and the instructors' teaching methods. That is why, technically, student ownership of the text can be considered irrelevant or at least less important at the classroom level than one might think, because faculty are measuring student and in-structor achievement. Theoretically, these voices are correct. When it comes to actual assessment practices, though, compositionists should not be so convinced of the student-centeredness in these dis-cussions. Far too frequently, we can read about and watch other in-structors at all grade levels and across the curriculum drive the criteria for what is "good" writing. Then the students' writing be-comes measured in a teacher-centered manner. Although these dis-cussions often result in well-intentioned actions and beliefs—such as how writing socializes individuals and affirms their membership in a community of scholars or thinkers - the conversations create a strain on the concepts of community and writing by trying to estab-lish a one-sided norm grounded in academic writing. In practice, what emerges is a focus solely on writing conventions, structure, grammar, and mechanics. Damn the ideas, unless the student writers are skilled enough to articulate their views in flawless standard American Edited English.

This approach promotes a double-bind circumstance. Critics of writing programs and of Composition in general can argue that writing instructors are blind to teaching critical thinking because their red pens keep marking up the content. Should compositionists put down their pens, these same critics can then wail that stan-dards are falling in the institution's writing program. Either way, the instructors take ownership of the students' work; in the first instance by virtue of a heavy hand and in the second situation by having to defend whatever their standards are for each class they teach. The ones who produce the text, the students, are rendered si-lent in both instances.

Although students do perform a task in a writing assessment context, whether it is a conventional or alternative assessment, how authentic can most assessments of learning be with a silent partner? To draw on a business metaphor, a practice that is now quite common in higher education, the silent partner invests most of the capital and often has the greatest risk in a joint venture. Yet the silent partner has no direct say in the active partners' transac-tions. The silent partner is indeed an owner, just one who has no voice or control. If we extend this idea to writing assessment as it is currently practiced, even in online situations, the student as silent partner is an owner of the text. She invests her intellectual capital and takes risks, perhaps even having the greatest risk in being graded, but when decisions and grade transactions are made by the other partners, the evaluating instructors, she is rendered wordless. The student's other partners decide for her the best course of action regarding her text—her intellectual property. Unlike the silent business partner, who can pull her capital if the active partners' actions run counter to the silent partner's, the student-as-silent-partner's property can be co-opted by the other partners without great regard for the student's intangibles in the writing process. But, to what extent should students be involved in an assessment? Is a reflective letter or statement or preface to one's work enough to give voice to the silent partner? And if the student owns his or her own words with regard to online contexts, as it seems court rulings indicate, what makes for an authentic assessment?

This last question becomes a thorny one if students truly do own their words in online communication in the writing classroom. Like formal education, computer technology also socializes writers in various communities and affirms their membership through language. Much like the idea of writing assessment, the computer also strains the notions of community and writing to reflect a collection of independent thoughts on e-mail, web sites, chat rooms, blogs, and MOOs. Unlike formal education and assessment, however, computer-inspired learning resists outcome objectives and goal direction. Rather than norm the literacy process, Internet culture puts the obligation on the user to gather, sort, and evaluate the information in front of her. If anywhere, this is the point where computer-based composition and current writing assessment practices are diametrically opposed: who owns the words the writer uses. At one time, the writer did. But, in cyberspace, as the reader scrolls screens and links, the reader owns the words. The reader clearly adopts and appropriates them for her own if she imports the words into her own text. When an e-text is evaluated, the instructor owns it as she makes her marks and annotations on screen. Similarly, anyone who accesses the student's e-text from elsewhere on the Internet can own the student's words by taking them and incorporating them into other e-textual forms. In each instance, the student's writing loses its connection to time (and sometimes to space) and becomes subject to greater integration of other texts, methods of inquiry, and instances of encounter, all of which confound traditional understandings of writing assessment as being a singular, individual effort that measures a singular student's achievement.

Earlier in the book I raised two questions that can now be addressed in this chapter: Can writing faculty evaluate written work that is completely owned by the students, particularly on a large-scale or a departmental setting, especially if an entire class develops into its own literate community and so understands the language, the contexts and texts, and the adaptability of the discourse to communicate with others? Or is the culture of Composition such that student writing will never be fully owned by its writers and will always have, to varying degrees, the teacher overriding or overwriting the final submission? To this, let me add a third question to be answered later in this chapter: Can technological convergence transform writing assessment into a more humane process?

CAN STUDENTS EVER FULLY CLAIM OWNERSHIP OF THEIR WRITTEN WORK IN NETWORKED CLASSROOM ENVIRONMENTS?

Convergence brings us new sets of techniques, knowledge, motivations to write, and skills that reflect multiple literacies that cut across lines of race, class, gender, and physical ability. The merging of these two technologies requires instructors to present writing differently and to evaluate it in some other way. Through technological convergence, language becomes a tool for both a writer's entertainment and her information. Lecturing is nearly eliminated, and students work collaboratively or independently on inquiry-based or problem-solving tasks. As such, college composition is simply no longer a process leading to a product; instead, writing becomes central to a communication system—a network filled with information, verbal play, resources, and discursive exchanges with others. Student writers come to see themselves as "information creators" (Wickliff, in Yancey & Weiser, 1997, p. 328) who use various literacies to solve very specific, pragmatic communication problems. Moreover, as the United States District Court in Lincoln, Nebraska, decided in 1998, students who write in networked spaces are published authors, because the web is considered a legal publication forum.

These points not only change the well-documented accounts of altering the classroom dynamic found in most articles about computers and their affect on student writing; they also question who really retains control over the text. Undoubtedly, this shift raises challenges not only to how instructors define their writing assessment practices but also to how writing instructors conduct the assessment. With the importance of visual rhetoric and the implications of having a global audience for one's class writing, clearly older theories and practices about what is or is not good writing are put into dispute in networked contexts.

Still, the questions of whether a student truly ever owns her own e-text and whether an instructor can evaluate effectively a student's e-texts haunt us. One of the promises implied in much of the early literature on computers and composition was that students would take more control and possession of their electronic texts. Since the mid-1980s, essay after essay in computers and composition literature has claimed that students become more empowered in their writing when introduced to online coursework. This idea has become more than a mantra in Composition; it has become a meme. This meme of student empowerment has extended to writing assessment as well, as following reflects a common claim: "Electronic portfolios support pedagogical goals of students' control over the organization of their portfolios and the kind of metacognitive awareness often associated with the reflective material found in traditional writers' portfolios" (Wickliff, in Yancey & Weiser, 1997, p. 337). But how is this done? Broadly painted statements like these occur throughout much of the computer and composition literature, but is "control over" the way a portfolio is organized or "metacognitive awareness" in reflection real student ownership of the text, whether it's in electronic or paper form?

Many writing teachers, including some of the leaders in e-portfolio use, still fall back on teacher-directed writing portfolios. Trent Batson, writing in *Syllabus Magazine* (December 2002), described his use of portfolios that compares with most teacher-directed models for portfolio use: Students collect their assignments and revise the best work until they whittle away to the finest writing they can produce. As Batson (2002) noted, the large web-education conglomerates like WebCT, Blackboard, SCT, and others are developing e-portfolio tools as add-ons to their course-in-a-box programs. What becomes apparent is that in each of these instances, the computer becomes little more than a gimmick for the same old writing assessment delivery systems of indirect evaluation through an instructor's establishing skill-and-drill exercises in these programs and holistic scoring of student work. Students are still the silent partners in writing assessment.

Even the most current, progressive ideas in computer-based writing instruction, such as students writing in hypertext, sound retrograde in this published example where the instructor outlines his project goals for a portfolio assignment:

> Before the first class was over, we began our semester-long discussion of the issues of diversity on campus and worked through the first of many drill and practice exercises in the Culp and Watkins *Educators' Guide to HyperCard*. The standards I set for the students' hypertexts were 1.) that they allow readers to contribute to the document in some way; 2.) that they incorporate graphics into the document; 3.) that they make some use of the audio capabilities of the Macintosh; and 4.) that they produce a document useful to other students and faculty. (Wickliff, in Yancey &Weiser, 1997, pp. 333–337)

Wickliff's published example, like so many unpublished ones, is symptomatic of how traditional assessment talk undermines total student ownership of the completed e-text. The language in Wickliff's essay is as authoritarian as any found in an ETS scoring rubric, and the first-day activities are as dry as any skill-and-drill practice approach. This instructor, like so many others, takes the notions of interactivity, visuality, perspective, and theory and reduces them to fixed entities. As Wickliff clearly noted, the critieria for the assignment are his, and his alone, even though the class is investigating diversity issues.

In further describing what transpired in his course, Wickliff (1997) explained the students' reflective memos. Even these were highly structured responses constructed around several issues the instructor developed. In this instance, the instructor reviewed the completed hypertext in much the same way another would evaluate a timed essay—holistically. Although Wickliff reported that his students remarked that they discovered a sense of ownership from working in hypertext (1997), how much of this ownership would these students have had if they shared more fully in the creation of the standards used to evaluate the finished text or if they had more freedom to experiment with hypertextual writing beyond the set drill and practice exercises and the rigid assignment outline put before them?

Gregory Wickliff's (1997) example is presented not to attack him but to show how tricky it is to blend the language and concepts from these two technologies. The language Wickliff used to structure his assignment's goals reflects an inherent dilemma with teaching in a networked environment: instructors becoming too much a cowriter in the students' work. Blair and Takayoshi outlined very well this problem of the instructor as cowriter in hypertext assignments:

> The text becomes our version of the text, depending on which direction we take our reading and on how much the writer involves us in our role as reader and coproducer. Thus, our evaluation becomes wrapped up in our creation of the portfolio as we make our choices in the reading. With the hypertext portfolio, the blurring of roles of reader and writer significantly blurs the evaluation process as well. (Yancey & Weiser, 1997, p. 365)

This is exactly what occurred with Wickliff's assignment. The students' hypertexts became his version of the e-text, particularly when he required students to include some way for readers to add to the document. With the roles of writer, reader, and evaluator blurred, how are we to know whether Wickliff (or any other instructor) offers a solid evaluation?

My concern is that too many writing teachers overwrite the students' work in these situations so that the students' e-texts conform more to the instructor's version of what an e-text should be. Too often, the hypertext or e-portfolio bears the professor's design more than the students'. The result is parallel to how younger students' science, math, or history projects sometimes reflect the influence of an all-too-eager parent who is willing to jump in and help complete the project. Blair and Takayoshi (1997) are right that compositionists who work in networked space must be aware of and able to negotiate their roles as reader and writer, because those tasks certainly fluctuate in electronic communication. However, Blair and Takayoshi's notion of writing teachers becoming coproducers of the students texts makes me uncomfortable. A coproducer is just that—one who creates the text simultaneously with another. For me, this type of thinking suggests that students will always be placed in the subaltern, apprentice, or silent role to the more educated, experienced reader and writer—the composition instructor—who acts as colonizer or master of the e-text in the classroom. Given that most students are so comfortable and familiar with technology and certain communities, they may be the more educated and experienced ones in the classroom. If student ownership of the text is a genuine goal, then why wouldn't instructors encourage this role reversal?

Nor am I sure that an active reader is an actual coproducer of the e-text in the ways Blair and Takayoshi (in Yancey & Weiser, 1997) suggest. Yes, in hypertext particularly, it is accurate to say that readers "write" as they link events in countless ways. But the composer of the hypertext document still constructs the links and images in multiple paths to lead readers through various readings of the text. Also, it is still the hypertext writer who determines the possible variations a reader can make. A similar point occurs with students writing HTML documents for web sites. The finished web site may be highly interactive and offer viewers innumerable perspectives regarding sensory and support items. However, the underlying HTML code is developed by the original writer and offers select options for the future reader, who then "writes" the document at a sitting. So, although the e-text reader may be an active one compared with traditional print forms, she may not be an authentic coproducer of the e-text.

The matters raised by Blair and Takayoshi (in Yancey & Weiser, 1997), as well as those elicited by Wickliff's language in assignment construction (in Yancey & Weiser, 1997), allude to why students do not always gain the ownership in their writing promised to them by computer-based composition. Because most compositionists still only recognize customary expository or argumentative forms in writing, the student writers' shift to a nonstandard or a mundane textual form—even if the student writer selects a most useful melding of genres for the context—leads to a corrective reaction from the more traditional writing teacher. Instructors' correctives may be anything from overcommenting on the material or hypercorrecting word choice, grammar usage, and other sentence-level errors to becoming a coproducer of the student's text. The correctives emerge when and if instructors perceive that the student writers are not somehow creating threads in the e-text that do not make meaning happen in predictable, learned ways. What arises in these situations is the conservative voice of writing assessment; the instructor's need and expectation to evaluate, to draw conclusions, about the text based on what can be normed or replicated.

Thus, the ownership issue of student e-texts is complicated by how instructors view students' work and student learning. Some compositionists see writing instruction as teaching sets of discrete, portable skills and strategies drawn from professionally written models. The result of this approach is students creating a "bag of tricks" they can dip into at will to construct a paper on demand. In this system, student writers are not considered to be "real" writers. They are apprentices learning the craft. Students do not own their work; they merely replicate what has been shown before. Proficiency is marked by how well student writers emulate the professionals and not by how well the students plan an original approach, organize it, negotiate the interplay between language and ideas, and revise. The difficulty with this pedagogical approach is not only its timeworn quality in light of the numerous advances in collaborative and constructivist teaching styles; it is also the problem that few professional models of hypertextual writing or other networked writing exist. Most online examples are created by nonprofessional writers or by folks who think of writing as an avocation or a way to communicate ideas with like-minded others. In short, most internetworked writing is produced by writers who are very much like our students. Students soon ascertain that they are just as proficient as the writers they emulate in networked space, and it becomes very easy for students to dismiss any instructor's evaluation of their work if the critique does not match the context in which the e-texts are produced.

For those instructors who value inventiveness and self-reliance in a writer's decision making more than the correctness of form, the issue of students owning their texts (electronic or paper) tends to be less a pedagogical concern. These teachers seem to have more an apprehension regarding how to evaluate a work that regularly resists current alphabetically literate understandings of what defines good writing. They understand that the definition of good writing varies, but the motives underlying what makes good writing reflect similar goals. Many of these compositionists look for patterns of risk that show a student writer's growth, watch for changes in the multiple literacies found in their students' networked writing that indicate development, and rely on classroom reflection to define how change occurs in each student writer as well as in their own teaching practices. In the face of mounting institutional pressure to devise quantifiable learning outcomes for their classes, however, these instructors are not always certain whether traditional assessment procedures are compatible with writing in a networked environment. More likely, these teachers find present assessment methods to be completely in opposition to the student writing development occurring in their computer-based classrooms. Generally, the assessment procedures in place tread heavily on a writer's choices, especially in large-scale approaches. These teachers find that assessment frequently limits interactivity, as the traditional rubrics preselect what characteristics a student writer is expected to demonstrate in the finished piece. All of this is antithetical to the tenet in computer-based writing that the more choices for a writer, the better to communicate with an audience. Moreover, these instructors recognize the rights of students to own their texts and make textual decisions—even in assessment situations—and this position often places them at loggerheads with others in their departments, their colleges, and in their communities who want to know why students nowadays can't write.

To repeat the question posed at the beginning of this section, Can students ever fully claim ownership of their written work in networked classroom environments? In most cases, no. The traditional classroom model of teacher overwriting or coproducing the text is too ingrained in most writing instructors' pedagogical training. Until composition pedagogy includes sections on how to work with student writers as genuine authors who have real rights in online writing, how to stop the grading hand from moving too quickly toward a text, and how writing assessment needs to conform to the purpose of the assignment, it seems that teachers overriding the students' texts will continue.

Likewise, it appears nearly impossible for writing specialists to ever fully evaluate an e-text that is completely owned by the student. If the student truly owns the text, she is guaranteed certain rights and privileges accorded to other authors. To be completely respectful of the student as author, the instructor will more than likely have to revise her assessment and teaching practices to reflect this change in the student writer's status. This is especially true in networked environments, where others' voices carry as much weight in assessing a student's finished piece as the instructor's. Writing specialists will have to renegotiate their role as single evaluator of the e-text to prevent overwriting and overriding the students' e-texts. The instructor's voice of the assessor is just one of many in this converged, interactive form of writing. Mechanisms can be put in place that allow others to respond to the students' e-texts, such as a pop-up response form to review the student's site or a short checklist with possible selections that visitors can tick to record their perceptions of the student's site or hypertext. Although the instructor can and should make comments, as should the class, outside readers should also be invited to read the work and respond to what they find. Something as simple as asking for external evaluations for e-texts moves current writing assessment practices toward the more authentic evaluations a "real" writer receives when submitting a paper for review. Moreover, this type of assessment tool offers a dialogic exchange between writers and readers and it shows writers how their work creates an identity in cyberspace and how others come to interpret this identity.

These little evaluative add-ons not only take the burden of assessment away from a single instructor; they also show students how various readers' needs are met. It is possible that small groups of teachers and students familiar with e-texts could share the process of evaluation, much like art or film departments conduct a day-long critique of student work. By providing a space in the actual text or site where people could access reviews of a student's work, writing faculty begin to educate others about what characteristics make a hypertext or a web site or a MOO or a blog good or poor. An archive of comments can be constructed as well, so students and instructors could return to various sites to study what respondents valued or rejected in the work. Creating an archive of comments accessible to students and instructors is an important step for avoiding what has been described as the "fictionalizing" of student writers in traditional portfolio contexts (Schuster, in Black, Daiker, Sommers, & Stygall, 1992, p. 319). Although a reflective narrative can still be constructed to explain the student writer's experience, this narrative is built on a series of comments analogous to the text and its production instead of on the students' personalities, classroom demeanors, or rhetorical skill in writing reflective letters. This seems to be the most workable way to establish an authentic assessment of student-owned e-texts that respects the rights of the students and the demands for learning outcomes that programs, departments, and institutions now expect for courses.

IS THE CULTURE OF COMPOSITION TOO RIGIDLY CONSTRUCTED TO ALLOW FOR COMPLETE STUDENT OWNERSHIP OF THE TEXT?

As someone who has studied and taught in Composition for more than 17 years, I want to believe Composition's culture is not so driven by instructors' control that full student ownership of the e-text is an impossibility. I also want to believe there are ways for compositionists to assess students' e-texts without overriding students' ownership. Although from reading accounts in the national newsweeklies and in the *Chronicle of Higher Education* these last few years, the present climate in higher education makes me think that students having complete responsibility for their e-texts, including a strong say in their assessment, is still in the far future. Writing faculty are seeing a greater emphasis on certification and accreditation on their campuses; with that type of attention to official legitimation in the learning process, thinking about writing assessment as being anything more than a rubber stamp frequently seems difficult. However, this current state of hypercertification in education should not prevent compositionists from envisioning what an enriched assessment plan—one that includes full student ownership of the e-text—could look like in the years ahead.

When Edward M. White discussed assessment and power in his book *Teaching and Assessing Writing* (1994), he offered two convincing claims: "If you really value it, you will assess it" and "What you assess is what you value" (pp. 292–293). Instructors who teach in computer- enhanced composition classrooms and who promote an evaluation plan that accommodates the principles and values of networked writing need to keep these points in mind. For Composition to shift its vision toward meaningful ways to measure writing development in a technology-enhanced environment, it will take scores of instructors— individually at the local level and collectively at the national level—to initiate conversations about those processes, characteristics, and purposes valued in e-texts. Part of that conversation must be how Composition can appraise electronic texts without relying on antiquated terms and beliefs.

Throughout this chapter and the book, readers will notice that the word *product* is never mentioned in relationship to students' electronic writing. This has been intentional. Composition still overvalues the product in evaluation settings even though the discourse centers on process. Holistic readings of essays and portfolios continue to focus on the "finished" pieces. Some institutions persist in requiring multiple-choice skill tests as barrier or placement exams. These events remain although Composition's dominant rhetoric over the last 25 years or so has been centered on process. To return to an old logical saw called the law of noncontradiction, something cannot be one thing and its opposite. Composition cannot say that writing teachers are focused on teaching process but assess on product and still be a valid method. The rhetoric and the practices need to be aligned.

The first stage in realigning writing assessment in an age of technological convergence is to realize that there are significant differences between pixelized texts and papertexts. When the expectations for literacy shifts from one primary source to a multitude of sources, as is the case with writing e-texts, writing specialists need to consider a complex range of institutional, curricular, instructional, and social elements involved that affect the assessment.

A model I want to present here is grounded in the work of Tim Peeples and Bill Hart-Davidson (in Allison, Bryant, & Hourigan, 1997). Peeples and Hart-Davidson offered a strong heuristic for approaching papertext assignments that account for various factors in the evaluation process. Their example addresses the four critical constraints—expertise, available artifacts, institutional–classroom limitations, and programmatic–curricular concerns—that affect how compositionists rate a text. To extend this idea to reflect the convergence between computers and assessment in the writing classroom, the following additions must be included:

1. Features of the "expert" writer in networked space
   - Is comfortable with using multiple electronic genres to suit various writing purposes
   - Has an awareness of and complies with diverse discourse conventions related to writing and responding to different discussion lists, chat, MOOs, and the like
   - Recognizes that knowledge in electronic environments is local and contingent and is constructed by the group in which the writer participates
   - Understands that each networked space maintains an epistemology, an ideology, a rhetorical structure, and subject positionality (cf. Howard, 1997)
2. What student grading artifacts are easily accessible to the instructor in networked space
   - List, chat, blog, or e-mail archives
   - Web sites students build
   - Hypertext or HyperCard projects
   - Databases students build
   - Electronic portfolios of individual student work

- Uploaded and electronically graded (holistically scored) student essays
3. Institutional or classroom limitations or issues that affect student performance
    - Institutional pressure to increase technology use or information literacy requirements in the writing classroom
    - No institutional support for increasing or maintaining technology across campus
    - Poorly configured or equipped computer labs or classrooms or no access to computer lab or class at all
    - Prior student experience with or access to computer equipment
4. Programmatic or curricular goals or concerns that affect student performance
    - Emphasis on collaborative work versus emphasis on individual as a producer of a product
    - Outcomes assessment driven versus instructor-developed assessment
    - Conflicting current–traditional versus social constructionist pedagogical philosophies in programs and departments or between teaching faculty
    - Widespread institutional support for computer-based composition versus limited or no support
5. Social contexts that can affect student performance
    - Racial, economic, or gender barriers that make technological access difficult for many student populations
    - Real or perceived societal push for all youth to gain technological skills
    - Current political climate that stresses accountability at all levels of instruction

Knowing the types of assessment and institutional situations in which faculty find themselves frequently helps instructors make better decisions and explanations for the grades or responses given to student work. As Peeples and Hart-Davidson (1997) suggested, instructors who envision themselves as participant-developers of student expertise in general instead of distanced evaluators of an individual's knowledge see a change in the instructor–student relationship.

This type of teacher understanding becomes important for acknowledging and promoting student authority and ownership in the writing classroom at levels that correspond to specific institutional and curricular goals. In the computer-enhanced classroom, this knowledge helps compositionists understand the marginalization that often occurs when an instructor's pedagogical practices are at odds with the institution's or the program's positions. Moreover, by thinking along the lines presented in the model mentioned earlier, faculty who use computers extensively in their courses and who teach at the fringes of their departments can discover how to frame their discussions regarding student assessment of online texts in ways that allow them flexibility without being considered too lenient or unorthodox in their standards.

Although this outlined approach probably will not increase teachers' adopting online methods for their own classes, neither will it stop institutional marginalization for many instructors who believe that teaching in computer-enhanced classes is the future. However, for junior faculty or future faculty in graduate schools who will soon face the tenure wars, using the model to frame arguments in recontracting and tenure packets could prevent the increasing denials of tenure and promotion for innovative, creative, progressive professors who find themselves unable to articulate what they do in their writing classes and how it meshes with or advances present institutional and programmatic goals.

In time, and with many voices from across the college curriculum joining in with those who now teach in computer-enhanced writing classes, the idea that genuine assessment requires more than the writing teacher's perspective will gain strength. Although this move doesn't suggest that grades, placement requirements, and barrier exams will be eliminated from either campus culture or Composition's culture, it does hold the hope that the students' role will be encouraged to grow in assessment contexts beyond establishing a few minimal criteria or writing reflective letters or memos after completing an assignment. Perhaps through Composition's coming to value electronic writing and the e-texts students create, an authentic assessment plan can develop that respects the rights of the author.

At the beginning of this chapter I asked who owns the words in writing assessment. If instructors examined the history of writing assessment, the answer would be obvious. The professor owned the words. Regardless of whether the measurement of a student's ability was grounded in indirect or direct holistic assessment models, the professor made the decisions. The professor could take that grading hand and override, overwrite, and overpower the students' words.

However, current discussions about assessment in Composition are moving toward discovering more humane, respectful, and localized ways to evaluate a range of student writing (Allison, Bryant, & Hourigan, 1997; Elbow, 1996; Faigley, Cherry, Jolliffe, and Skinner, 1986; Huot, 2002; Yancey & Weiser, 1997; Zak & Weaver, 1998). These discussions are a start, as the language of assessment now sounds somewhat more democratic than in its earlier phases at the beginning of the 20th century. Now, Composition's culture at least uses the rhetoric of process—and in some circles, the rhetoric of postprocess—to discuss how to evaluate e-texts. Although much more needs to be done in this area to put the rhetoric into widespread practice, these voices have pushed us away from the behaviorist-based products like the Intelligent Essay Assessor and other such predicate analysis or key-word-in-context programs to evaluate student writing. Instead, writing specialists began online assessment with the electronic portfolio, as Batson noted (2002). In the following chapters, several models of evaluation are presented that suggest convergence can and will transform writing assessment practices as well as offer students the respect they deserve as authors who own their own words.

Chapter 4

Rethinking Validity and Reliability in the Age of Convergence

The commonsense notion in Composition Studies is to create assessment strategies that correspond to our pedagogical practices. When writing teachers use the traditional quantitative understandings of validity and reliability to evaluate their students' e-texts, instructors are doing the opposite of what past wisdom suggests. New methods and processes in technology, similar to new methods and processes in the teaching of writing, require users to reexamine older practices that measure how far, how fast, or how accurate is the recent change. Often this reweighing of earlier ways comes from inaccuracies discovered during an evaluation, from a shift in perspective that allows a different view to emerge, or from more information learned over time. For writing assessment in an age of convergence, all three possibilities contribute to the importance of rethinking the old standby concepts of validity and reliability to address students' written competence because computers have provided a (r)evolutionary movement in the teaching of writing.

Validity and reliability are the two epistemiological cornerstones of assessment, this much writing teachers know. Because reliability is easier to define, let me start there. Simply put, *reliability* refers to the ability to consistently give the same answer at different points in time. Reliability depends on three factors: the stability of a result to withstand time, the internal consistency of performance along a scale, and the ability of two parallel forms to measure the same concept (Wimmer & Dominick, 1997, pp. 54–55).[1]

Validity frequently is defined as whether a test measures what it is supposed to measure. There are many, many other forms of validity that can affect an assessment, however. Evaluators look to see whether a test has face validity, predictive validity, concurrent validity, and construct validity to determine whether a test's questions gauge the information fairly for what the question asks of the respondent (Wimmer & Dominick, 1997, pp. 55–56). More precisely in performance situations, such as a writing exam, validity addresses the significance of test scores. Samuel Messick, of ETS, following educational researcher L. J. Cronbach's view of test validation, stated that

> these scores are a function not only of the items or stimulus conditions but also of the persons responding as well as the context of the assessment. In particular, what needs to be valid is the meaning or interpretation of the scores as well as any implications for action that this meaning entails. (1989, p. 15)

Generally speaking, for most genuine writing evaluation circumstances, validity is not a totalizing situation; validity depends on the evaluators' skill in judging whether an item measures what it is supposed to. Even Messick (1989) supported this position. For Messick, va-

---

[1]Briefly, following Wimmer and Dominick's explanations (1997, pp. 55–56), *face validity* describes whether on the face of an exam or an assignment the question measures what it is supposed to measure. *Predictive validity* examines an assessment instrument against a future outcome. In writing assessment, if a multiple-choice exam on grammar can predict the success of students in a first-year composition (FYC) course because the exam correlated positively with passing scores in FYC, then faculty can say that the exam has high predictive validity even though the face validity is extremely low. This is because the multiple-choice exam is not testing the student writing, only a subset of skills. *Concurrent validity* evaluates how a measurement tool performs against an established criterion. For instance, if writing teachers wanted to gauge the validity of an editing exam, they could administer the exam to a group of professional copyeditors and a group of students. As Wimmer and Dominick noted, if the exam shows a clear discrimination between the two groups (and, of course, it should based on predictive ability), then faculty can claim that the editing exam has concurrent validity. *Construct validity* connects the measurement tool to a theoretical structure to show a connection related to other items in the structure. Linking this idea to composition classes, an assessment instrument needs to relate to the program's or the instructor's pedagogical practices to indicate there is some relation between what is being measured and other variables in the course. The converse here is also possible: An assessment method can have construct validity if it does not relate to other variables in the course or if there is no theoretical or pedagogical reason for a relationship to exist. *System validity* describes the process that the exam or evaluation has to a larger structure, such as a writing curriculum or institution, to ensure that what is being assessed bears a relation to the state goals outlined by a program, department, or institution.

lidity, like reliability, involves "social values that have meaning and force whenever evaluative judgments and decisions are made" (1989, p. 17). So to some degree, validity is a subjective interpretative process. Because of the social value and subjective aspects of validity, there is an inherently political side to validating a student writer's ability.

What makes Composition's use of validity and reliability particularly problematic is etymology. The terms *validity* and *reliability* are historically grounded in the scientific approach to knowledge and knowledge making, as well as the psychometric approach to test measurement, which assumes several conditions for the composing process:

- *Writing is orderly and can be regulated.* In the scientific method, all actions and events happen in a regular, orderly manner. Even when an environment is under great change and rapid fluctuation, scientists presume there is still a degree of order that can be observed under any condition.
- *Writing is a knowable object.* The assumption that anyone can "know" writing is without proof. However, test and measurement practitioners who follow the scientific method argue that writers, like other natural objects that exist in the world and have unique characteristics, can be understood and their actions explained by the same methods used to study other natural phenomena.
- *All writing has natural causes.* *Natural* in the scientific sense means not rooted in fundamentally religious, supernatural, or magical forces. Once an object is determined to be natural, then a cause-and-effect relation can be discerned. Depending on one's personal or cultural philosophy, this statement can be debated.
- *Writing is drawn from the acquisition of experiences.* In the scientific approach, writing is empirical because it relies on perceptions, experience, and observations. Individuals' perceptions arise from sensory and abstract situations. Moreover, experiences give rise to a knowledge base, as interactions with the physical and social world affect one's perceptions. Observations allow persons to make generalizations, speculations, and inferences based on earlier perceptions and experiences.

Therefore, the epistemic principles of validity and reliability in writing assessment will create a sense of understanding about writing using a methodology based on an arrangement of clear, normed rules and procedures. These rules and procedures construct a system of evaluation that permits ordered observations, inferences, generalizations, predictions, and analyses. Yet, as Messick and educational researcher M. T. Kane have indicated, the resultant scores that emerge from these evaluation systems supposedly connect to "relevant content and operative processes" that are "presumed to be reflected in scores that concatenate responses in domain-appropriate ways and are generalizable across a range of tasks, settings and occasions" (Nachmias & Nachmias, 1981, p. 145). However, what happens far more often is that the interpretations and actions derived from the scores are "typically extrapolated beyond the test context on the basis of documented or presumed relationships with nontest behaviors and anticipated outcomes or consequences" (Nachmias & Nachmias, 1981, p. 146).

As with most things, in practice, ideas such as validity and reliability are more complex than they are simple—particularly when the concepts are applied to something with as many variables and issues as writing. Writing specialists need to understand that an assessment tool has to be evaluated against other characteristics to conclude its worth as a measurement instrument. Assessment instruments are only useful when they are both reliable and valid, and far too often in something like the evaluation of real writing outside of highly constrained test conditions, the chance for attaining solid confidence levels for validity and reliability is nearly impossible.

Now, I'll concede that some assessment proponents might differ with my observations. These individuals will argue that holistic essay scoring and portfolio reading have depended on behaviorism's recognition of validity and reliability for decades to offer credibility. If real validity and reliability exist in these situations, though, it is usually because the students' test conditions provide a veneer on the process that tricks teachers, departments, and institutions into thinking and believing that their exam is reliable and valid. Let me argue here that most writing assessment instruments are unreliable for several reasons, from students misunderstanding the prompt's wording or its expectations to instability in students' responses (which could be a sign of growth or cheating instead of an error, but only in clearcut cases is one ever quite sure) to a lack of internal consistency to a problem with intercoder reliability (commonly called "splits" in holistic readings). In the language of tests and measurements, these lapses are called *variable errors* because the "error varies from one observation to the next and also because the error is different each time it is measured" (Lauer & Asher, 1988, p. 140). Rarely will a writing assessment tool give a consistent, stable, equivalent result, which is what evaluators look for in a reliable measurement instrument because too many variable errors have the potential to exist each time an evaluation opportunity occurs. Composition researchers Janice Lauer and William Asher (1988) noted that the precision of the criteria, the amount and quality of the procedures used in evaluator training, the continual monitoring of readers during an evaluation session, the speed of rating, and the readers' background and attitudes all affect reliability. To that list, in the age of convergence, writing teachers can now add the medium used to produce the text.

Writing programs that depend on stability in their assessment instrument scores may not be accurately evaluating their student writers. Usually, group stability in a writing assessment is virtually nil, as I have tried to show, which is what writing instructors should expect. After all, if stability occurs in a student's assessment over time, then growth has not occurred. For this reason, writing specialists should tread carefully if they are basing their assessment instrument's reliability on its stability in an exam environment. This is even more concern for caution if the student is working with new technological media to write the exam. Student writers' abilities can and do change over time, especially with their facility in using computer programs. Assess students' skills too soon or too long a period after introducing new material or software, and false results can occur. If faculty are expecting stability to happen with the test, a student's higher score on a second round may not necessarily indicate a flaw in the testing tool. Other variables, such as greater or lesser comfort levels with composing on screen or the students' familiarity with the software program, can make a difference in student scores.

Given the difficulties regarding variable errors, consistency of results is also difficult to maintain in a writing assessment. In the psychometric model, consistency in assessment should not turn up any conflicting elements. For instance, a consistent reader is expected to read in accordance with other readers. Or a writer is expected to make consistent errors or possess a consistent style on the task. Of course, writing instructors know that consistency in assessment is also subject to error. Any change in genre can expose different writing errors or a shift in voice, tone, or word choice.

Certain types of assignments—such as argumentative writing—create more errors in students' writing because of the increased demands the activity places on the thinking and information-gathering processes and because ecological or individualistic fallacies that teachers have about writing interfere with readers' abilities to make decisions on many of these pieces.[2]

Equivalence frequently causes problems in writing assessment, which affects an assessment's reliability. As Lauer and Asher (1988) described equivalency reliability, two sets of test scores given simultaneously to a sampling of people are correlated to each other. All aspects of the data must be the same (equivalent), such as the averages, standard deviations, and average intercorrelations among items before running a correlation of the data. Although equivalence works well with a standardized, indirect writing test, the problem arises with holistic readings of essays and portfolios, because the data across two assessment settings may not be equivalent based on variable error. It is entirely possible to have differing averages, standard deviations, and average intercorrelations among items that can skew correlations.

Validity is also a problem for writing mechanisms because of errors caused by the lack of face validity. This is simple error in that the test does not measure what it appears to measure on the surface of the test. But other problems for validity exist as well. The inability of a testing instrument—whether testing indirect or direct writing—to predict a student's future success in writing can also affect some forms of validity. So can unstated criteria used to pretest the assessment mechanism affect some aspects of validity. Moreover, validity can also be affected by the lack of connecting an essay, portfolio, or multiple-choice exam to any departmental or pedagogical framework.

Too often writing faculty and their departments go for the easy form of validity, face validity, as their defense against other prob-

---

[2]In empirical research, an *ecological fallacy* refers to using aggregate data that help to analyze a group to make inferences on the behavior or properties of an individual or individuals. For example, in a holistic reading (portfolio or essay structure), applying gender or racial statistical data for the campus or the region to assess an individual student's work would be using an ecological fallacy. The opposite of an ecological fallacy is the *individualistic fallacy*. In this situation, a reader makes inferences about an entire group of students or an educational system in general on the basis of a single student's work. An example of this would be condemning all high school writing instruction on the basis of one student's writing sample. See Nachmias and Nachmias (1981, p. 57) for a social scientist's perspective on these two fallacies.

lems in the assessment mechanism. The difficulty with this practice is that an evaluation tool can have face validity and be completely invalid in the more important areas of tests and measurements. Of course, when many compositionists realize this point—generally when they are in some administrative or other across-the-campus meeting—the results are sometimes less than amiable. Writing faculty need to be aware that problems of validity frequently occur in assessment because writing is an indirect process, and, if educational researchers are truthful about the subject, no one is totally certain that what is being measured in a piece of writing is precisely what is intended to be measured. This is not a flaw with the teaching faculty or the students' achievements in the class; this is a condition of trying to evaluate the unknowable—that is, how each person creates a written product. After all, there are significant connections to craft and to aesthetics in writing, and those variables cannot be measured objectively and quantified.

How validity and reliability have been presented in writing assessment, especially in writing assessment that is post–indirect method, reflects the language of an earlier, psychometric understanding of writing. For psychometricians, writing can be reduced to discrete variables addressed by multiple choice quantifiers. So, it makes sense that terms applicable to quantifiable research be used to describe evaluation. Composition, writing instructors should hope, has moved beyond this point. In the last 25 years, the field of Composition Studies has progressed in the direction of qualitative and action research methodology in both its scholarship and assessment philosophies. The advent of poststructuralism and postmodernism ushered in social constructivism, ethnography, content analysis, and discourse analysis—none of which paralleled the quantitative processes. Consequently, changes have occurred in the ways in which writing assessment is conducted. Holistic scoring, in principle, corresponds to the qualitative researcher's belief that writing cannot be divided into subparts and the entire work must be looked at as a whole unit. However, to mollify the psychometricians, holistic scoring in writing has numerous subsets and criteria that do indeed divide the students' work into pieces. These subsets and criteria form the rubrics that teachers use regularly in evaluating writing.

Similarly, portfolios also correspond to the qualitative position that writing can be assessed only after students engage in an intensive, lengthy involvement working with a series of texts. Instructors can only evaluate students' writing after the instructors observe the changes that are noted through teacher and peer comments, student reflection, or other types of documented evidence. The reporting of results during an assessment includes detailed explanations, commentary, and more layers of reflection. Yet usually, portfolios are read holistically based on some sort of rubric that segments writing. Moreover, portfolios are increasingly subjected to the breaking out of criteria in a barrier exam format. Therefore, what instructors find is that even a more qualitative form of assessment like portfolios can be transformed into the language and actions associated with the psychometric model.

Because most composition specialists now try to create a very different reality concerning writing assessment compared with the psychometricians' methods, one has to ask, why is Composition still using the definitions from an antiquated approach to describe and explain the changes that occur in student writing? As Brian Huot (2002) noted, because Composition never truly claimed writing assessment as part of its domain, there is no reason for the field to attempt to reclaim or rearticulate the psychometricians' discourse. With the great influx of computer-enhanced writing classes, this question is particularly salient, and it clearly affects what happens in the college writing curriculum. Not only does the blending of assessment technology and computer technology reconfigure classroom space and instructional techniques, students' perceptions of their authorial rights, and the characteristics of the text; it also affects how compositionists study their students' finished work. These older rubrics and concepts are a poor fit for the multiple layers of composing that happen in networked assignments because they have accounted for neither visual rhetoric nor the development of the types of content and the variations of style that exist in electronic texts.

Writing instructors must realize that quantitative and qualitative methodologies ask faculty to view the individual writer in distinct ways; the quantifier sees the student writer as one of many, and she places the writer in categories that correspond to general observations about behaviors, attitudes, and expectations. The qualifier looks at students as independent beings, each one possessing very different sets of abilities, and assessment cannot group these abilities into nice, neatly separated categories. This separate worldview toward assessment leads to the quantifier needing large numbers of students to satisfy an explanation of what is happening in the writing classroom and the qualifier to prefer smaller numbers of students to provide a general pattern of activities in a composition class. What is significant about this point is that writing departments are now filled with readers from both camps and each side reads student papers. Although assessment indeed drives instruction, recognizing that assessment can be defined through two opposite theoretical approaches illustrates the fissures that can occur in departments regarding written evaluation as well as the rifts that emerge in pedagogy.

The schism that seems to exist in writing assessment practices from program to program, perhaps even from instructor to instructor, mirrors Composition's mistrust of assessment. Few practitioners and scholars understand tests and measurements, as Brian Huot (2002) rightly noted. Even fewer recognize that Composition is not bound to quantitative definitions of concepts like validity and reliability to describe what occurs in the classroom. It is possible to reconfigure these terms to accommodate the flexibility necessary to discuss the writing process in networked writing classes and to do so without causing great conflict with social constructivist pedagogical models. The way to realign validity and reliability in writing assessment in these computer-enhanced contexts is to think even more qualitatively about evaluation.

University of Michigan education professor Pamela A. Moss, in her research on accountable assessment with portfolios (1992), indicated that frequently a student writer's growth is made evident by examining the qualitative aspects of the writing. For instance, having instructors look at the increasing levels of complexity in student problem solving often reveals that there is a loss of control in mechanics or organization as student writers develop richer interpretations of a text. According to Moss (1992), there are other subtle indicators of growth like quality of voice and elaboration. These characteristics tend to be understated in psychometric approaches and subsumed under broader criteria, which causes faculty to miss or to misinterpret critical moments of a writer's development.

In thinking qualitatively about writing assessment in networked environments, instructors are asked to consider depth instead of comprehensiveness in evaluation. This means that instead of collecting webfolios or electronically generated assignments from everyone in the class, teachers work with smaller representative samples of each assignment to examine what happens in the course over time. In the process, a theory of instruction that is situated to the course and to the institution develops. Not only is approaching writing assessment from this perspective more in line with Composition's interest in cooperative writing, ethnography, protocols, and discourse analysis, but the inductive method of inquiry common to qualitative research also parallels more closely a writer's composing activities. From a practical standpoint when working in internetworked spaces, qualitative assessment helps faculty construct categories of incidents or events that happen in students' online writing processes that then can be refined and examined for patterns or themes to describe various relations among the multiple literacies and activities in the class. Once the preliminary connections are made, instructors can integrate the information into a coherent explanation of what transpires in the computer- enhanced classroom using a theoretical framework that corresponds with their teaching philosophies.

Even in the more quantitative instructional design and development circles, qualitative methods are now thought of as having some validity and reliability compared with a decade or so ago. This is particularly so when qualitative approaches are used to triangulate student test scores or to discuss specific student populations. This suggests that there is enough of a precedent set in research design for qualitative assessment to be valid in all writing classes. To have qualitative writing assessment data stand alone and maintain validity and reliability without statistical support, however, a level of confidence must be created for quantitative folks to respond favorably to the data put before them.

For those who teach in computer-enhanced classrooms, this point is especially important. I don't mean to scare writing instructors, but new electronic essay-reading software programs that imitate variations of the ETS holistic scoring process or the predicate analysis method found in the Intelligent Essay Assessor are gaining publicity. These programs can easily become the type of representation quantitative researchers recognize as acceptable writing assessment mechanisms for networked writing classes. The administrative appeal for these systems is understandable; low-cost, high-volume production that speaks in statistically accurate language. To counter such a regressive approach to writing evaluation, though, compositionists and their program heads need to consider what qualitative techniques offer writing assessment that is better and more dependable for their institution's needs.

Currently, electronic portfolios are the first foray into qualitative methods applied to writing assessment procedures for online classes. This move is based on the success that the common papertext portfolio has had. Over the last 25 years, the traditional paper portfolio has gained value as a valid and reliable application for assessing student writing. Therefore, it makes sense to import the idea into networked classrooms. However, as noted earlier, the same difficulties that exist with paper portfolios also exist with electronic portfolios. Selective pieces may be overwritten by faculty or outsiders; only individual teachers or a team of teachers completes the evaluation process; fictionalizing—or maybe overextending—the writer's abilities occurs because of clever reflective texts, or in the case of e-texts, because of stronger visual literacy skills or pixel manipulation; and the focus of evaluation still rests primarily on product instead of process. All this becomes apparent in many current computer-based writing assessment plans like the one W. Dees Stallings presented to new teachers in his monograph *Distance Education* (1997). Although Stallings is correct in suggesting that subjective and objective criteria are critical for providing effective writing assessment in computer-enhanced composition classes, his model is based on traditional primary trait analysis combined with an analytic scoring guide (1997, pp. 26–27). Although rubrics like these work for standard academic writing assignments, and will work for the standard writing assignment submitted to an instructor as an electronic file or in a webfolio, they fall far short of addressing the qualities of interactivity, usability, and visuality that are the hallmarks of e-texts. Instead, Stallings' use of assessment checklists and scoring guides reinforces current–traditional approaches to electronic writing instruction—and the students' products still remain at the forefront of evaluation.

Authentic assessment in the networked classroom space must account for more than finished work that can be accessed online. It should also include the public e-mails and chat exchanges, student commentary from drafts composed in software programs like WebCT or BlackBoard, or other nonfinished communication among the class participants. Generally speaking, e-portfolios do not contain this material, although they should. As Douglas Hesse recently noted, these informal, conversational pieces when threaded together in an archive form an "essayistic artifact" (1999, p. 38)—a local narrative that presents a history of the course work that does not appear in the portfolio. An essayistic artifact like a class's listserv archive becomes important in evaluation to examine how student writers develop a consciousness about their assignments and how students' various rhetorical and structural movements toward writing a longer e-text unfold over the course of an assignment. It makes sense for writing teachers to include a document like a listserv archive in an electronic assessment to account for change and growth in students' writing, yet how many compositionists do this? Not many—if any at all. From the various e-portfolio samples I've seen as online representatives for conducting an evaluation of networked writing, no links exist to a list archive. In fact, most student webfolios look like digitized versions of the common paper portfolio—something that Batson (2002) encouraged. This suggests that writing faculty may be missing rich sources of qualitative data to support assessment decisions.

Evaluation discussions must also extend to design and content concerns in more formal web documents. There are clear differences between writing online and writing on paper, as outlined in chapter 2. Authentic assessment for internetworked writing has to account for the changes in style that occur when students create mundane e-texts. There can no longer be face validity connected to e-texts because writing instructors can no longer rely on assessing only the surface structures of their students' online assignments. More comprehensive feedback mechanisms need to be created to explain to students and to skeptical faculty members and administrators that real writing happens in electronic classroom spaces.

DEVELOPING "DEEP ASSESSMENT"

Because technological convergence brings changes to the text and to the students' writing processes, it becomes critical for writing instructors who are interested in pursuing computer-enhanced composition classes to contemplate alternative assessment strategies beyond those that already exist. These newer strategies have to build on the flexibility found in portfolios, be manageable enough to incorporate into an active writing classroom, be able to address a full range of formal and informal networked writing contexts, and be concise enough to appease administrators and other officials who typically understand quantitative data. Although this idea sounds utopian, it is not. Instead of examining the dilemma of evaluation from its traditional tests and measurement roots, writing instructors can look to a more congruent area for communication convergence—the media. Compositionists can find innovative avenues of critique and commentary in media research that can transform older notions of writing assessment without sacrificing validity and reliability.

One new way to think about writing assessment in networked environments is what I call "deep assessment." Deep assessment arises from the work of two different compositionists writing almost a decade apart, Margaret Himley (1991) and Ann Watts Failliotet (1999). The concept underlying deep assessment emerges from Himley's "deep viewing" techniques (1991) that were applied to children's writing. In 1999, Pailliotet adapted deep viewing to accommodate critique of visual and electronic texts. In the deep assessment approach, I modify Pailliotet's (1999) and Himley's (1991) ideas to initiate a postmodern turn in the evaluation of writing.

As with deep viewing, deep assessment reflects a three-tiered approach. Together, teachers and students, as participant observers, amass multiple data sources and artifacts that lead to describing elements of the texts. These descriptions form the basis for responses and interpretations of what is found in the texts. Whether in teams that divide the responsibilities of deep evaluation or as single evaluators, the instructors write comments, notations, or sketches about the material in front of them as talk begins about each selection. This talk unfolds into interconnected discussion, and the written comments emerge as the artifacts that concretize the evaluators' exchanges.

TWO STRATEGIES FOR IMPLEMENTING DEEP ASSESSMENT

Using qualitative research to invert the traditional meanings of validity and reliability in assessment is important for documenting the evolution of writing and writing instruction that takes place when extensive computer use is introduced to the composition classroom experience. Because computer-enhanced writing instruction is frequently a fluid series of exchanges among writers and because the products that arise from networked classes are frequently seamless and without closure, the deep assessment mechanisms used to study these students' work must have great flexibility. In addition, any assessment strategies for these contexts need to have some common ground with the historical understanding of validity and reliability to gain the respect of the quantitative folks who generally sit in decision-making capacities on campus and who frequently deride any measurement system that does not look like a numeric study.

One method for building credibility in deep assessment is to develop what is called in media research an *analytic induction strategy* (Wimmer & Dominick, 1997). In this technique, the evaluator forms a hybrid between quantitative and qualitative research methods. The first step in this strategy is for the assessment team or the instructor to state clearly the criteria to be investigated and to construct a hypothesis to guide the evaluation procedure. Next, the instructor pulls a representative sample from the entire group of students using a commonly recognized random sampling formula like "1 in X." For an instructor who teaches four sections of composition (approximately 100 students), she can use her class lists to select a 1 in 10 sample to pull 10 students' electronic assignments at random to study further. Then she can examine a single case from the representative sample to test the hypothesis. If problems occur in the evaluation, she reworks the hypothesis or the criteria and tests again. Otherwise, she judges the remaining cases from the representative sample, looking for patterns and themes that refine her hypothesis. When finished, the teacher returns to the 10 sample assignments to study any negative cases that could disprove her hypothesis. If problems occur, the instructor again reworks the hypothesis and continues testing. Although this is a time-consuming activity, the teacher should develop a very strong argument that maintains elements of quantitative and qualitative assessment. Moreover, this inductive and recursive evaluation method has credence in other academic communities; numerous educational researchers, for instance, find this form of naturalistic inquiry to be a valid form of accountability (Hopkins, 1998). This becomes important if a faculty member or a program must present harder data to administrators or faculty senates to support curriculum matters.

A second, somewhat less labor-intensive, way of building a deep assessment context that is credible without relying on historical understandings of validity and reliability also comes from media research. Maykut and Morehouse (1994) proposed four conditions for establishing trustworthiness in reporting qualitative data. Here I have adapted Maykut and Morehouse's 1994 model for use in a writing assessment situation:

1. *Collect data from numerous sources.* Student e-texts, protocols, e-mail exchanges, listserv archives, and other classroom artifacts show others that the evaluator studied the students' work from many perspectives. This content does not necessarily have to be in an electronic portfolio; in fact, a polished e-portfolio may hinder the study. An electronic portfolio does not provide the raw information needed for the evaluator to truly measure growth and change in the student writers' processes. A few "finished" pieces might be useful, but instructors should have a mix of work in various stages, genres, and contexts for more believability in the evaluation.

2. *Develop an audit trail.* Whether in a LAN space, or on a disk, CD, or keychain hard drive, teachers need to create a safe, permanent record of the class's original data, comments about the data, and any analytical methods used to conduct the assessment. This permanent record is called an "audit trail." Audit trails are the easiest way to demonstrate the possibility of replication in qualitative research. Audit trails are especially important when arguing the validity of an assessment procedure, as anyone can retrace an instructor's steps and check the results for accuracy. An audit trail for 10 students may take up to several kilobytes in a single assessment, though, so instructors might want to consider putting this information on some removable, easily stored, permanent system (rewriteable CD-ROM or DVD, for instance) if they do not have access to their campus network or if the bandwidth exceeds campus allocations.

3. *Conduct member checks.* As teachers make notes and develop conclusions about what they read, those on the assessment team review their findings with each other and with the students to ensure accuracy in reporting the material. This step is very important if instructors use protocol interviews with students, because teachers will want to be certain that they precisely capture the students' words and intentions.

4. *Develop an assessment team to avoid epoche.* In research speak, *epoche* means researcher bias or prejudice. Establishing a team of evaluators to keep everyone focused on the criteria when describing

or interpreting the student samples helps reduce the potential for bias. Sometimes it is helpful to bring in an evaluator from outside the composition classes to serve as an external reader whose primary function is to keep everyone honest in her assessment of the work. For instance, in a networked writing class that has hypertexts or web sites as part of the class work, the assessment team might include a willing faculty member from the computer science or art departments who could lend his or her expertise if needed. This person could observe the process and raise questions of possible bias or misinterpretation of the work should the situation arise.

5. *Apply deep viewing approach to the data.*

These two methods are workable for instructors and are fairly nonintrusive for students. Students can and should be involved with the data collection beyond the gathering of completed student assignments, particularly in the deep viewing sections of the evaluation. Protocol interviews, reflective statements, video or audiotapes of sessions, comments from students about the stages of their work, and their reactions to instructor responses are all necessary components of qualitative assessment and are common data-collection techniques in composition studies. Including student participation in the assessment activities acknowledges students' authority as writers in a legitimate way that respects their interests and stakes in the writing and evaluating processes. This move is an especially important one when assignments are cooperatively written, because students have already invested a high level of ownership in the formation of their work. Furthermore, to exclude a range of student responses or critiques (or only to include student reflections) in online assessment contexts seems to me to be antithetical to the democratizing rhetoric underlying computer-enhanced composition pedagogy. It suggests that the teacher still holds the only authoritative position in the classroom, and the student writers' voices carry little weight. Without student input, the assessment would not be considered deep nor would it be as democratic as many in Composition hope writing assessment could be.

THREE MOVES TOWARD DEEP ASSESSMENT: THE ONLINE LEARNING RECORD, TOPIC/ICON, AND DYNAMIC CRITERIA MAPPING

The Online Learning Record at the University of Texas at Austin is an excellent bridge between using conventional writing assessment plans and deeply evaluating students' writing in electronic contexts. Recently, Margaret Syverson and John Slatin created the Online Learning Record (OLR), the first public inroad toward deep assessment that moves beyond the electronic portfolio (see www.crwl. utexas.edu/~syverson/olr/contents.html for an overview of the system). Although the OLR has been designed primarily for the K–12 writing teacher, it can be adapted for the college or university writing instructor. The OLR contains many principles expressed in this chapter; it fosters student participation in the evaluation process, draws evaluation artifacts from several different sources, accounts for the range of multiple literacies needed to write in networked spaces, and traces students' progress graphically instead of numerically or alphabetically. Moreover, the OLR allows instructors to construct narratives or visual tracks regarding student work that reflect teacher accountability and respect for the students' efforts in the classroom. Syverson and Slatin's OLR model (1999) points to the positive effects that technological convergence brings to writing assessment by illustrating how humane and democratic evaluation can be in a composition course.

The OLR's greatest benefit is that instructors now can follow student progress rather than focus on the product. Through various forms of graphical plotting, writing specialists can track students' perceptions of growth and change without the stigma of grades. This is a critical step in realizing an authentic assessment program for computer-enhanced writing classes, because many students still come to these courses with the fear of technology. By reducing much of the grading to a series of sliding bar scales and scattergrams, the instructor can observe how various students rise and fall in relation to certain challenges in writing for electronic environments. Final grades still exist, as do individual assignment grades, but the numeric or alphabetic distinction given to students now carries an observable history, a context for understanding why students receive the grades they do in a course.

What is also impressive about the OLRs that, although retaining some of the usual quantitative representations for data like sliding bar scales and scatterplots, the information gathered is highly qualitative. Because data are gathered from numerous sources, including archived files, current projects, and student observations and reflections of their growth as writers, an audit trail can be easily built with graphical dimensions to discuss writing development in a systematic manner. Thus, a teacher can reach the most quantitative and qualitative members of a campus-wide study group, instructional design team, or administrative committee interested in how writing is affected by technological convergence. Over time, these audit trails establish a rich, generalizable body of knowledge about a particular student population (or, for large- scale assessment, an entire class of students).

As a way to deeply assess the writing activities and abilities of students in interactive settings while retaining student ownership of the written product, the OLR addresses five important stages: (a) building writers' confidence and independence, (b) acquiring skills and strategies, (c) monitoring levels of prior and emerging experience, (d) using writing and inquiry as ways of knowing and understanding, (e) developing critical reflection (Syverson, 1999). For these reasons, in OLR the evaluation better situates itself in the shifting contexts of the computer-enhanced writing classroom because it depends far less on the one-dimensional approach to measurement found in skill-and-drill work or the two-dimensional procedures like "competence and confidence" grounded in much of the current holistic essay and portfolio reading models that form the basis of other computer-driven assessment tools.

The OLR is still in its infancy, and it is used in a limited manner at the K–12 level in California and at the university level at the University of Texas at Austin. Despite its newness, the OLR's early phases indicate that Composition's convergence with competing technologies can lead to developing a transformative assessment practice that combines independent inquiry, ability, student ownership, limited teacher intervention, and critical knowledge about situated discourse. As the OLR concept spreads and evolves, more compositionists and administrators should see first-hand the effect that deep assessment and convergence have for the teaching of writing at the K–college level.

In fall 2002, Fred Kemp at Texas Tech University (TTU) instituted the TOPIC/ICON program to handle the writing evaluation for TTU's 2,250 students in first-year composition. Given the size of TTU's program, the sheer volume of information collected in TOPIC/ICON's database would have to be enormous. According to the TOPIC/ICON web site (www.english.ttu.edu:5555/manual), the database holds more than 180,000 student documents. Clearly, in one semester, TTU has built a massive foundation from which to mine information about students' online writing activities and behaviors.

However, it is not the mammoth database that makes TOPIC/ICON worthy of recognition in the blending of networked writing and assessment. Rather, the openness with which TTU conducts this deep assessment procedure is estimable. All stakeholders involved in the assessment process are able to obtain critical information when it is needed. Students have access, both public and password-protected, to a variety of class-generated information. Instructors have access to various classroom management tools and archives, all fairly automated for ease of use. Program administrators have access to important section statistics at their fingertips when statistics are needed to answer questions or to solve problems. The accessibility to data that all participants have in the TOPIC/ICON system demonstrates that it is possible to create a writing assessment plan that merges two technologies and provides responsibilities to everyone involved in the learning process.

One might think the TOPIC/ICON system would be cumbersome given its size, but it is a model for efficiency. The TTU faculty involved in building TOPIC/ICON have redesigned the roles of instructor, dividing the work load into two separate activities: classroom management and document evaluation. Consequently, there are classroom instructors and document instructors. Classroom instructors direct classroom learning. Document instructors maintain responsibility for evaluation and commentary on student work. The division of labor here is important, because it becomes incredibly grueling for instructors to act as classroom manager, motivator, writing coach, and final arbiter of student work while teaching in networked space. Separating the practices allows instructors to gravitate to their strengths. For universities with large graduate teaching staffs or adjunct faculty, this option offers better programmatic control over the quality of instruction in that writing specialists who have a better presence in the classroom or who are more experienced with students can have the burden of grading removed. Those who are exceptional readers of student texts but who may falter in the classroom because of their lack of graduate or teaching experience can do their best as well as gain a stronger background in working with student texts. With this system, it is easy to set up a rotating teaching schedule so all instructors eventually spend time either in the classroom or on evaluation. Therefore, the work load is shared by everyone, and a coordination of best practices in the teaching and assessing of writing can emerge.

The planning of the TOPIC/ICON program reflects the deep assessment model presented earlier in this chapter in several significant ways. First, the program collects data from numerous sources and places the information in databases or archives that allow stakeholders easy access. Second, the databases and archives establish a strong audit trail for administrators and instructors. Third, the writing program administrator is able to conduct member checks through the program administrator's functions. Fourth, the TOPIC/ICON planners attempt to avoid epoche through the establishment of working groups that read student papers. Additionally, TOPIC/ICON values not only the pedagogical needs of students in a computer-enhanced writing class but also the instrumental and affective needs of both students and instructors in the assessment process.

This last point is evidenced most clearly when one reviews the criticisms posted to the public. From the students' perspective, their concerns were similar to those in any first-year writing class: papers too long for instructors to grade, classes that did not seem rigorous enough, and instructors not prepared enough in using the technology (www.english.ttu.edu:5555/manual). The instructors' issues were the same as many humanities professors who are teaching elsewhere. Technology dehumanizes the class experience. Students seem ill-prepared to work with the TOPIC system. Grading papers takes forever. If the reader did not realize she was reading about a course that is a hybrid of computer and F2F contexts, she would have thought the end-of-term comments came from a completely classroom-centered situation with some computer component attached. Therefore, it seems that in the TOPIC/ICON system, merging these two technologies does not drastically alter students' or instructors' perceptions of the work load attached to first-year composition. What the comments do suggest strongly, though, is that students and faculty need time to familiarize themselves with any new technology if the system is to be truly successful.

Like the OLR, the TOPIC/ICON approach is the next wave in large-scale university writing assessment that does not rely on either a one-shot electronically scored essay or an e-portfolio for deep assessment. Both the OLR and TOPIC/ICON programs put forward an exciting next step in the development of deep assessment strategies that recognize shared responsibilities in the networked writing classroom. Furthermore, TOPIC/ICON constructs a prototype for what larger writing programs can do to be more efficient in delivering course content in an age of technological convergence. At the K–12 level, OLR demonstrates a similar effectiveness in working with younger students' writing. What the OLR and TOPIC/ICON systems show compositionists is that deep assessment of networked writing can occur in very different forms to meet various institutional needs. Composition does not have to be dependent on older understandings of writing assessment to offer legitimate evaluation methods for electronic texts. It is possible for writing specialists to construct new assessment models that draw on the two technologies and still acknowledge validity and reliability, albeit in ways that break away from Composition's past.

Bob Broad proposed a fresh idea with regard to writing assessment that shows potential for working with electronic texts. In his book *What We Really Value* (2003), Broad detailed the Dynamic Criteria Map (DCM). The DCM is a series of circular regions, some linked, others not, that address varying textual qualities. Two regions, Change in Student/Author and Rhetorical, are linked through Broad's "epistemic spectrum" (2003, p. 40). Changes in Student/Author are marked by growth in learning and in revision, whereas the Rhetorical region is defined by audience awareness and persuasive abilities.

Broad ranked the epistemic spectrum as the "most substantial criterion" in the model, because it positions affective and moral thinking, epistemic knowledge, and intellectual analysis along a continuum that bisects the Change in Student/Author and Rhetorical constellations (2003, p. 40). An offshoot constellation, Aesthetics, that reflects criteria dependent upon the writer's craft (texture, creativity, humor, etc.), links to both the Change cluster and the epistemic knowledge range of the continuum.

The DCM also includes assessment criteria clusters regarding Agency/Power (author as writer) that intersects with Ethos (author as person) and a discrete area defined as "part to whole," which houses the structural elements of writing such as focus, pace, relevance, clarity, flow, and so on (Broad, 2003, p. 40). Two smaller compartments, "mystery criterion" and "general writing ability," are set apart from the larger domains.

The appeal of the DCM for e-texts is in how the model addresses a full complement of writing needs. Regardless of whether the electronic text is a blog, a MOO, a web site, or hypertext, the work can be evaluated on a full range of technical, mechanical, aesthetic, affective, rhetorical, intellectual, and social criteria defined by the instructor, the program, or the department. Broad's DCM system depends on the deep assessment approach put forward earlier in this chapter in order to collect and discuss student networked writing in a thoughtful manner. Through an instructor's use of the DCM, students can chart their progress in various areas and note where growth and slippage occur across assignments or over time. For a program or a department, the adoption of a model like the DCM provides the context in which to discuss the evaluation of students' electronic texts to enact curricular or instructional changes that improve writing instruction for networked environments. As I propose in the next section, the DCM approach leads Composition Studies to redefine validity and reliability in ways that mesh with the growing use of e-texts in the writing classroom.

DEVELOPING A "NEW" VALIDITY AND RELIABILITY

The notion of deep assessment and the development of deep assessment programs like the OLR, TOPIC/ICON, and DCM is that they replace the flat, objectivist descriptions of validity and reliability with an enriched overview of the students' real processes and contexts for writing. One critical effect of technological convergence on assessment is the destabilization of the scientific method used to ground writing assessment by the computer's ability to emphasize the social values and subjectivity present in evaluation. This destabilizing of established understandings inherent in the scientific method surely changes how writing undergoes evaluation.

A start in this new direction for assessment begins with a revised set of assumptions concerning writing, validity, and reliability. In place of the older principles that guide assessment and were outlined earlier in this chapter, a new collection of components drives evaluations in computer-enhanced writing courses:

- *Writing is multidimensional.* The convergence of these two technologies has displaced the earlier concept that writing is an orderly and regular activity. Hypertext, MOOs, Daedalus Integrated Writing Environment (DIWE), and archives of synchronous and asynchronous e-mails indicate that writing runs across different geographical spaces and time zones; accommodates multiple topics, users, and sources; and fragments into short bursts with the addition of graphical images and hyperlinks. What has happened to writing with the cross-impact of technological convergence is a process of deterritorializing words from their preestablished orders. Electronic forms of writing now mirror what theorists Gilles Deleuze and Felix Guattari (1987) called a rhizomatic linguistic structure. That is, writing no longer maintains a distinct, three-part split among the world, the text, and the author. Instead, different aspects of perception allow different connections to be made; however, there is no genuine start or finish to the writing. In Composition's technological convergence, writing is multidimensional because it is always placed in the middle of things, positioned between visual images and sound or between the actions of the writer and the reader.

- *Writing is an observable process.* What specifically triggers writing is unknowable; also, explaining how a student writer achieved a particular outcome from examining a single sample or a series of written products outside of the classroom context is equally unknowable. However, technological convergence makes a student author's processes observable even though the product is seamless. Therefore, instructors in computer-enhanced courses can conduct nonintrusive evaluation beginning with the students' first forays in networked writing. The assessment becomes increasingly more authentic, because students are expected to contribute to the evaluation process through a series of analytical activities based on their own work. Thus, teachers' online archives become a rich, longitudinal source of metacognition and metawriting as well as a database for students' technical competence and writing effectiveness. Although writing specialists are still unable to know what exactly initiates the sequence a writer takes in the composing process, through a rich archival database, instructors can observe the stages that online composition takes once the spark occurs.

- *Writing is one form of many situated discourses.* Instead of privileging alphabetic literacy and papertexts, technological convergence provides strong evidence that writing is just one discursive activity and knowledge maker among others. Albeit writing is still a central communication method in e-texts, writing now includes graphical interfaces, hybridized oral and written language patterns, sound and video applets, and a range of reader–writer interactivity. Internetworked writing exists in a very different format compared with the historical pen-and-paper forms that many instructors have come to recognize. Although writers and readers still have to manage the meaning, intent, structure, and effect with e-texts, the volume of associations, connections, and evidence that needs to be constructed for the prior experiences and literacy levels of a global audience is expanded at least a hundred-fold. So, although writing is a central activity, it emerges as one of many discourses available to a writer in online environments.

- *Writing reflects social exchanges influenced by numerous causes.* Convergence in Composition reinforces Kenneth Bruffee's claim that "knowledge is a consensus" and "people construct independently by talking together" (1993, p. 113). In networked classroom environments, there are several sources for affecting the outcomes of the types of social exchanges that exist among writers (adapted from Bruffee, 1993, pp. 116–117):

  Levels of technical knowledge or interest

  Levels of shared expertise or common information base

  Patterns of argument and approval (e.g., ad hominem, flames, use of narration vs. citation, "dittos," short supportive slogans, etc.)

  Patterns of reward ("cool site awards" or other markers of web site excellence, permission to publish list comments, friendly emoticons in posts)

  Acts of competition (verbal sparring, one-upping, leveling, and the like)

  Levels of trust and comfort (e.g., lurking vs. regular contributions to lists)

The writing done in networked situations, then, serves in some way to embody all those who are connected, that is, to act as a medium to express private thoughts publicly with those who are of similar minds. This is an important aspect of what technological convergence brings to the writing process; it makes visible the social relationships that writers attempt to establish with their audiences. In these contexts, just as Bruffee (1993) noted happens in all collaborative contexts, writers validate their beliefs through each other. Therefore, online assessment that is collaborative will have a deeper effect on students because they will measure the worth of their writing based on the types of response received.

- *Writing depends on experiences, values, and technological access.* Those who were alive during earlier periods of technological convergence in writing cannot tell today's writing specialists of the massive changes in experience that occurred when letters pushed aside speech or when the printing press revolutionized hand-lettered texts. From reading rhetoricians, historians, and scholars across the ages, one can only imagine or try to envision the transformations each moment in convergence had for society then and how those instances altered people's experiences, literacy levels, values, and access to technology.

We are, however, living in the most current wave of technological convergence. With our own eyes, many writing specialists see first-hand the triumphs and challenges that this critical moment in convergence brings to literacy. As more writing tasks shift from pen and paper to electronic type, students' experiences with composing the written word evolve. Most compositionists can recall one student (or possibly several students) or one class that had advanced cases of technophobia on the first day of class in a computer lab. Through trial and error, questioning, and a mix of confusion and confidence, these students arrive at a point where hypertextual or HTML composing, e-mail or ICQ ('I seek you") correspondence, PowerPoint presentations, MOO writing, or producing other electronically based assignments becomes second nature. What we discover is that writing in networked environments, like other forms of writing experiences, depends on students encountering the opportunity to practice on a regular basis.

With these newer assumptions about writing and the writing process in the culture of Composition, modifications must occur regarding the concepts of validity and reliability. Currently, as educational theorist William L. Smith noted, standard assessment methods assume too much both of the rater's ability for consensus on rating points and of the accuracy of the rating scales' intervals (in Huot & Williamson, 1993). Smith proposed a turn to *adequacy*, particularly in placement situations, to evaluate student work. Assessing for adequacy does not depend on extensive rater training or calibration of sample essays or texts; rather, the function of assessing for adequacy parallels the tasks of manuscript reviewers. The reviewers, chosen from members of a community, depend on their experiences with the material in front of them (in this instance, sets of student data archived online), to "accept, reject, or revise and submit (substantial revision or minor revision needed before decision reached)" (in Huot & Williamson, 1993, p. 198). In assessing for adequacy, students may learn to be more rigorous in showing competency compared with more traditional assessment settings. This is because assessing for adequacy looks at students' real writing abilities instead of measuring them against a generalized, idealized norm of written competence. Broad's DCM model (2003) points us toward a highly workable manner of assessing for adequacy in that the criteria are localized for a series of courses, a set program, or an institution based on the shared beliefs of the stakeholders involved with the evaluation.

Because archived data can be included in this type of evaluation, assessing for adequacy also allows for multidimensional plotting of student progress, takes responding to a student's work out of the linear numerical order that often substitutes for a grade, and presents responses in narrative (qualitative) forms that make better sense to students, faculty committees, and program administrators who may be unskilled or uncomfortable with quantitative research methods and statistical evidence. The ability to measure writing in this manner puts forward the position that the evaluators know the community in which the writer writes and that they can be fairer in their judgments about the material based on the evaluators' prior experience with teaching similar courses and students' prior experiences with writing in similar courses. Moreover, assessing for adequacy respects the local conditions of the institution where a student produces her assignments.

Smith's adequacy model is a reliable form of assessment for use with e-texts because the categories (variables) from which an evaluator selects a decision are limited enough to produce clear, consistent decisions. In assessing for adequacy, writing specialists simply measure whether the writing is acceptable for the situation. If the student's writing is not acceptable, the distinction becomes whether more revision is needed or whether the problems are severe enough to reject the piece completely. For networked writing composed of many components, literacies, and rhetorical strategies, assessing for adequacy is ideal. Instructors familiar with electronic communication can distinguish acceptable work in ways that break from the linear holistic scoring guides, yet still retain the sense of reliability that many test-and-measurement people want to see in outcomes assessment.

This "new" reliability does not depend on the consistency of writing specialists guessing the same score to keep consensus and interrater reliability or to ensure the reliability of test instrument, two situations that frequently lead to a Panopticon of sorts in assessment settings. Instead, this new reliability insists on faculty reviewers who are experienced with the currency of technological convergence and student e-texts to make decisions about the adequacy of students' writing in these genres.

Assessing for adequacy moves deep assessment closer to validity because the evaluators have the opportunity to examine a fuller scope of the students' writing activities and contexts. Not only will the archived data contain numerous examples of writing produced under various conditions and for various audiences, the students' own analytical examinations of their work and the instructors' points of intervention; the data should also reflect the teacher's comments. All these elements provide the breadth needed to make a valid writing assessment. Deciding whether a student's archived writing is acceptable depending on local criteria should pass the test for face validity because the data are evaluated by local experts using familiar criteria to measure the writing. Additionally, when a panel or team of teachers who are experienced in electronic communication evaluates the students' adequacy as writers of online material, there is also predictive validity. That suggests that evaluators acknowledge the students are reasonably able to do the work again later based on examining the archived materials. Concurrent validity can be included in this type of evaluation if the assessment team wants to measure the students' electronic writing against students' F2F writing; this approach might be an especially useful step in writing programs where there are computer-only sections (and, conversely, F2F-only sections). Testing for concurrent validity will be useful only if the criteria used to measure the writing remain identical for both sections. It is also important to note that in programs where computer-enhanced composition is under fire or where there is great skepticism, testing for concurrent validity may answer administrators' or faculty members concerns about the benefits of using computer technology in the writing classroom.

Last, deeply assessing writing for adequacy meets the demands for establishing construct validity. Because evaluators can link a theoretical framework to the assessment mechanism—in this instance, the body of information existing about writing in networked space, the growing collections in visual rhetoric, or the work done in media literacy describing the effect of media convergence on alphabetic literacy—the results become even more valid. The assessment team can explain the relations between what happens in the students' e-texts and other variables that exist in the theories being applied to study the writing. Providing construct validity in deep assessment reflects a more authentic assessment experience because not only are instructors evaluating what they value in an e-text, but the assignments and activities also demonstrate to students and observers what is valued in a text or a course. Applying construct validity in deep assessment respects both the students' development of multiple literacies through the writing process and the writing instructors' judgment that students can perform a cluster of writing tasks in cyberspace.

Technological convergence has transformed the text. Of that, most have no doubt. Writing instructors who work in computer-enhanced classes recognize that there is a range of modifications that occur in the writing process when students shift their composing practices from pen, paper, and an implied audience to keyboard, screen, and an actual audience. To make others across departments, campus, and society realize that these changes happen in students' assessment as well, compositionists familiar with these two technologies must transform assessment, because that is the language of administrators, university boards of trustees, and state legislatures. Collectively, compositionists who have expertise in computers and writing assessment must argue that deep assessment of students' online writing reflects the ultimate performance-based assessment for the following reasons:

- Instructors can examine complex learning outcomes and student abilities in writing beyond traditional pen-and-paper assignments.
- The focus of assessment is placed on process, which is critical for students' finished projects to function properly (e.g., graphics appearing correctly in web sites, Java applets that run and do not crash a user's machine, MOO sites that carry out an

activity, simple discussion lists that run most of the time without failure, etc.).

- The emphasis on process and deep assessment offers a more plausible, direct, and complete study of the types of literacies, reasoning, and techniques writers use to communicate online with real audiences.
- Infusing the composition course with computer-enhanced writing activities motivates students to write, because genuine readers exist for their work.
- Online writing is "real world" writing even though it takes place in virtual spaces.
- Like other forms of authentic performance assessment, deep assessment demands greater instructor time, involvement, and effort to collect, code, and analyze the data.

Outcomes assessment is possible, and maybe even desirable, in writing classrooms where convergence has taken place. However, fair outcomes assessment of networked writing cannot happen as long as older notions of validity and reliability are used to measure a nonquantifiable, nonstandard writing experience. These new intellectual projects come with the demand for developing suitable assessment criteria and models that address the range of students' processes, knowledges, and motivations when composing e-texts. Without writing instructors rethinking the psychometric concepts of validity and reliability in the age of convergence, Composition Studies will become severely constrained and this will lead to an even greater gap between classroom practices and evaluation. If the commonsense beliefs about assessment and instruction still hold true, then it is time that Composition redefines such central terms to reflect the broader aims of literacy in the electronic classroom and the changing shapes of the electronic text. We are on the cusp of changing the nature of writing assessment in the age of technological convergence; however, more work needs to be done. To do nothing further limits innovative pedagogical practices, the possibility of new scholarship, and the social values inherent in multiple literacies to the political whims of administrators, pundits, philanthropists, and policymakers.

Chapter 5

Hot and Cool Technologies in the Age of Convergence: Assessing the Writing in Room 25

Room 25 houses one of my department's writing labs. Some semesters I spend an incredible amount of time there, teaching classes like Writing for Electronic Communities, Writing, Research, and Technology, and Information Architecture. Other semesters, the students in my College Composition II classes spend hours in the lab or elsewhere, logging in and writing online.

There are days when I spend hours working with many students who have multiple levels of technophobia as well as with many students who are writing averse (sometimes the two groups overlap). From those moments, my thinking about the use of technology in the writing classroom has evolved. When I finished graduate school more than a decade ago, the technologies connected to writing assessment seemed to be cold and distant, a sure-fire way to alienate students in the composition classroom. Computer technologies, though, were "hot." In the late 1980s and early 1990s, those boxes of lights and wires and networks sitting in a writing lab were exciting enough to bring the most resistant student writer to class. Those days clearly are over. With wireless technology, with online classes, with increasingly mandated assessment plans, resistant writers have many ways to duck out of a writing class—even the required writing classes. Still, the McLuhanesque idea of "hot" and "cool" technologies intrigued me and made me wonder about how computers and assessment related to what was happening in my classroom.

As I investigated the notion of hot and cool technologies through theorists like Jean Baudrillard, Gilles Deleuze and Felix Guattari, and Paul Virilio, a revolution occurred in my teaching. What was once hot and cool became inverted for me, and a greater understanding of how these technologies function in writing instruction emerged. A complete change of pedagogical methods and the conditions I want to teach under came forward through my process of engaging with students, theory, and these two technologies.

COMING TO TERMS WITH HOT AND COOL TECHNOLOGIES

I have come to understand the conventional technology found in writing assessment as being a hot technology. Postmodern theorist Jean Baudrillard (1990) described this type of technology using Marshall McLuhan's term *hot*—a context that depends on influence, challenge, *mise en scene*, and spectacle. A hot technology is fraught with both direct emotional charge and high stakes, and it draws attention to vernacular use in print (McLuhan, 1964). As it is usually enacted in writing programs, assessment qualifies as a hot technological form because of the politics and economics inherent in language use that are regularly tied to evaluation and to the direct connections that assessment maintains with instruction. Frequently, there is a level of spectacle connected to high-stakes assessment situations that drive emotional reactions from teachers and students.

Borrowing from Baudrillard (1990), in a hot assessment environment, writing is generally defined in terms of the coherence and use of correct structural and mechanical forms, grammatical functions as well as rhetorical ones, and models instead of vernacular usage. Regarding the particulars of writing classroom practices and assessment, a hot technology imposes on the writer a reason to communicate. For example, two such areas where the imposition occurs in writing assessment are instructors providing rigid classroom assignments or exam prompts and teaching rhetorical techniques that match up with the exit test or portfolio. In these instances, students are not expected to think or develop ideas outside of the dictated formats. These students are not given the responsibilities of becoming a writer.

The spectacle arises at the end of each semester or quarter, when compositionists across the nation administer various types of barrier exams or portfolio readings in either first-year composition or at the rising junior level. The spectacle increases at the K–12 level with the state and federal mandates under the No Child Left Behind Act, and this spectacular event carries significant memories with students when they attend college. All too regularly, students consider these spectacular moments to be an unbearable hurdle rather than a measure of their writing abilities. Time and again, students view these large-scale, high-stakes assessment situations as a game subject to rules that students do not always understand or do not see the purposes of. Just as often, writing instructors do not always understand or do not see the purposes for why such an assessment must occur. As McLuhan (1964) noted, a hot technology has all types of consumerist and nationalist connections, which also seem to appear when writing instructors closely examine many mandated assessment practices. These consumerist and nationalist connections tend to infuse themselves into the purpose of the assessment itself, which deviates from the real intent of writing assessment. Although it might be beneficial to explain to students (and to faculty) all the underlying social, political, and economic concerns associated between writing and assessment to help them grasp the rules and purposes related to the spectacle, the reverse might happen. Writing instructors more likely would convince themselves that the writing test they are about to administer falls short of testing a particular domain of interest—in this case, writing competency—and does more to foster some kind of cultural unity or economic marker. Students most likely would become even more cynical about the value of writing assessment and take the event less seriously than many do right now. Neither situation bodes well for assessment.

Conversely, writing generated with the assistance of the computer is, in both Baudrillard's (1990) and McLuhan's (1964) view, "cool": a technology that requires modulation and deliberate infusion of the phatic function of language to communicate. For those unfamiliar with the concept of phatic communication, this term refers to discourse strategies that open lines of communication. Small talk, underlife discussions, exchanges regarding the weather or sports teams, or any other accepted established rules for beginning or ending conversations are categorized as being phatic. In conversations, phatic discourse creates rapport, breaks the ice in new conversational contexts, or concludes a discussion. For networked conversations, phatic communication is used to encourage postings or longer term discussions on a topic.

Instead of instructors imposing reasons for communicating with others, cool technologies depend on each writer seeking out the need to make linguistic contact with others. This is one reason why so many of our students' postings to lists or blogs display greater amounts of phatic communication compared with what instructors might want or hope for in a traditional classroom discussion. Cool technologies require individual writers to "restore the functional possibility of communication" and "to inject contact, establish connections, and speak tirelessly simply in order to render language possible" (McLuhan, 1964, p. 164). As a result, the phatic discourse structures help students move into networked discussions or writing. This type of communication lessens the possibility for spectacle occurring as well, because students are constructing an environment that adapts to their use of language.

The potential for spectacle also diminishes with the use of cool technology because monitor screens, terminals, laptops, and the like distance writers from the immediacy of writing on paper (the *modulation* that Baudrillard, 1990, addressed). These effects reduce the attention connected to the writer's use of language. Along with providing their words, writers using cool technologies can provide different viewpoints by adding images, hyperlinks, movie or video clips, or audio sound bites to adjust a reader's perceptions. The stakes in evaluation seem less significant with cool technologies because the writer's words alone are not being judged—the writer's words are always connected to other textual elements that mediate the response. As a result, cool technologies allow the writer to always be in collaboration with another writer or reader. Furthermore, as we have seen since the mid-1990s, networked writing knows neither cultural nor political boundaries in their traditional forms, so there is little concern with vernacular versus "proper" language use. All that becomes important is the infinite exchange of ideas and information among participants.

Writing with computers, then, becomes a ludic event, that is, a "play of models with their ever-changing combinations" where all combinations "can act as counter-evidence" for what is written and communicated (Baudrillard, 1990, p. 157). If writing specialists adapt Baudrillard's observations to the use of technologies in Composition, ludic writing becomes a supple, circular, and polyvalent method of communication. In turn, the coolness of computer technology presses the writer to initiate and continue communication with others in an effort to keep in contact; thus, e-mail messages, fragmented chat discussions, blogs, and hypertextually linked stories end the concept of totality prevalent in hot technology. The fragmentation of online writing creates a greater desire for writers to establish and maintain discussion, to be seduced by the instantaneous exchanges of information and talk on the screens in front of them, instead of conforming to the standards and conventions of something like academic writing.

As one of my College Composition II Honors students discovered during her spring 1999 research paper project, the seduction of instantaneous, continual communication can overwhelm a writer. This student, whom I will call Jane, found herself captivated by Instant Messenger, a "finger" program installed on the campus-wide computer system. On completing her paper and a corresponding web site, Jane described her dissatisfaction with both projects in her self-assessment letter. She explained her temptation to spend hours on Instant Messenger (IM) instead of on her writing assignments. Jane was seduced by IM's lure of continual communication with others, and she forgot her responsibilities to her work. Jane knew her finished assignments were not of good quality because of this distraction, and she now warns other students how easy it is for their attention to be diverted by a constant flow of messages. As a graduating senior, Jane now advises most of her peers to turn off this feature whenever they are working on an important assignment.

Student writers are not alone in succumbing to cool technology's enticement, though. Writing instructors also are tempted into teaching with computers through a number of avenues, from professional journals whose articles praise the rise of students' skills to university administrations that promise grants, release time, and even publicity of the professor's efforts. It seems as though everything connected to computers and composition appears interesting, reinspires students' and teachers' passions toward writing, and implies that the computer is the destiny of writing instruction. That is, however, until it is time to evaluate the students' work. At that point, as with most seductions, reality emerges: There are no ordered, established, or recognized ways to measure students' progress in cyberspace. What I found regarding the merging of hot and cool technologies is that convergence sometimes produces a luke-warm response in the classroom. Colleagues were curious, but skeptical, as to what I was doing with any assessment procedures that addressed online writing. "Too hard and time-consuming to be useful," said some. "Interesting. But the results are not generalizable enough," said others. "Stay with the portfolio idea," a small faction argued. "It's a tried-and-true method."

Coming to terms with the blending of hot and cool technologies means that compositionists need to seek out what elements of each technology work with the other form and with the instructor's own pedagogical philosophies, because these two technologies conflict more often than they coincide. Instructors also need to discover how phatic communication strategies function in academic settings, so as not to misread students' efforts.

From teaching the students in Room 25 and observing how they interact with each other and with the world, I have realized that my values for what makes writing and instruction "good" have shifted greatly. Seven years ago when I started teaching more extensively in Room 25, I would have probably argued that good writing is situated in specific contexts and purposes as well as is grounded in sound fundamentals. Good writing instruction helps students learn what techniques and strategies best address these multiple situations. However, today, I offer those who ask me a very different understanding of what good writing is. After teaching in Room 25, I discovered that computer-enhanced writing depends on the following:

- Textual constructions that invite and include readers more than exclude them
- Interactivity that moves beyond the semantic content of words into the use of typography, punctuation, color, and so on
- Language use that continually begs for additional communication among correspondents (often phatic forms of communication)
- Maintaining a consciousness regarding different cultural models and biases in visual, aural and linguistic representations and reflecting multiple levels of meaning
- Establishing *synthesia*, the interplay of the senses, in language use and mechanics that appeals to and send messages to both readers' ears and eyes as well as encourages tactile responses through linking, clicking, or pressing buttons

These reformulated principles of good writing now both redefine and reinforce my pedagogical stance. Because my graduate training was steeped in the radical–critical pedagogy movement of Freire, Giroux, Shor, Apple, McLaren, and others, my immediate classroom concerns are to always create democratic, problem-solving environments in which students learn by posing ideas and solutions that address an issue. Yet the radical–critical educator in me tends to be skeptical, if not entirely pessimistic, about the benefits of media and media technology in society. Although technology brings the world closer together, the old global village concept of McLuhan (1964), it also fosters forms of consumerism, nationalism, and colonialism that balkanize people. I must admit that sometimes it is difficult for teachers to determine whether all this technology helps or hinders students' literacy development.

Since I have delved into computer-enhanced composition instruction, however, my cynicism about the uses for technology in writing education has been tempered. Although I still find many of the discussions centered around the use of computers in the writing classroom to lean toward either propaganda or evangelism, the majority of radical–critical teachers' strident positions against the ludic writing found in much of cyberdiscourse is equally disturbing to me. Spending time in Room 25 watching my students enact in their writing and in their classroom behaviors many of the core tenets of radical–critical pedagogy[1] forced me to rethink how my teaching philosophy could mesh with—according to the literature, anyway—seemingly oppositional concepts like assessment and

---

[1]For those unfamiliar with the underlying ideas in radical–critical pedagogy, Pamela Annas of the Boston Women's Teachers group defined 16 points that outline the characteristics of a "radicalteacher." Instead of citing each aspect of what makes a radicalteacher, let me provide a brief summary of the main concepts. Radicalteachers are nonauthoritarian, information-sharing, respectful, reflective individuals who possess a set of social commitments and assumptions about the world and their subject area. Additionally, these teachers are good listeners and are not afraid of the sound of students' silence in their classes. Theory and practice, as well as process and product, are equally important and integral in students' learning. Likewise, students' mental, material, and emotional conditions are integrated in their willingness to learn—regardless of the students' race, ethnicity, social background, sexual orientation, or physical ability. Although concerned for the students' well-being, radicalteachers are demanding of their students and refuse to accept passivity or obedient, dutiful, nonquestioning behaviors in the classroom. Finally, radicalteachers realize that there is much they do not know about life, their subject, and the ways in which the world works—that is why it is important to question, to investigate, to challenge. For a more in-depth discussion of "radicalteaching," see Pamela Annas' *New Words: A Postrevolutionary Dictionary* (2004).

computer technology. Learning how to square the dual rhetorical strains of corporatism and democratization that run through technological convergence is a challenge to even the most self-aware, critically reflective instructor. I know this challenge happened to me more times than not in the last half decade. Many times I catch myself observing my classes and thinking of the Internet as "the familiar encrustation of images that accompanies any holy war, whether mandala, marriage of heaven and hell, World Wrestling Federation, religious icon, American Gladiators, or the matching bibs and banners of the medieval Crusaders" (Joyce, 2001, p. 57). As I watch my students compose online in web formats, I wonder how much of this writing is democratic and how much of it is corporatism run amok. Even though we study electronic civil disobedience movements, critiques of cybersociety, and the like in my classes, I find myself raising this question: Is it possible for teachers in a technological environment to separate out the democracy from the nationalism and the corporatism that exist in cyberspace? I have yet to come up with an answer for this, but it is a question that vexes me each time I teach in internetworked spaces.

The results of my trials and errors over the last 6 years have helped me form the following considerations for initiating transformative learning and assessment through the use of computer-enhanced composition. I offer them here as a way to consider new avenues for redefining literacy in the 21st century:

- Online communication facilitates a sense of community among students faster than most F2F classroom or teacher-initiated activities.
- Computer-enhanced writing instruction is purely holistic in the best sense of the word. Process is equal to product in the teaching of writing in networked spaces, and students' minds and bodies are engaged in solving the problems that arise in the action of communication. Students can also incorporate all their lived experiences and choices in their writing.
- In networked classrooms, information is shared across terminals and across the globe rather than across a teacher's desk.
- Learning and writing in a networked classroom space make students more aware of the disparity in racial, gender, sexuality, and economic issues in society than does discussing these concerns in a traditional classroom environment.

- On a regular basis, students display more knowledge about a wider range of subjects than their professor has or expects the students to know.

Assessment practices in computer-enhanced classrooms, then, require something more than an emphasis on skill or the manipulation of rhetorical techniques. Assessment also has to extend beyond the instructors' knowledge bases, because there are students who have greater knowledge in some topic areas and perhaps an even greater knowledge in technical ability. Moreover, writing assessment designed to accommodate a growing institutional push toward adopting computer-enhanced composition classes no longer has to continue on a consumerist, colonialistic, nationalistic, or corporatist path over who controls language use. Instead, technological convergence can offer instructors the opportunities to focus on the independent and collective writing processes of our students as well as the democratic use of information. The question is, Can any of this be achieved through the convergence of two distinct technologies used in the writing classroom?

DEVELOPING ASSESSMENT PRACTICES THAT ENCOURAGE THE BEST OF HOT AND COOL TECHNOLOGIES IN THE COMPUTER-ENHANCED CLASSROOM: SUBVERTING THE LAW OF SUPPRESSION OF RADICAL POTENTIAL

Media theorist and University of Wales journalism professor Brian Winston invented the phrase "law of suppression of radical potential" (1998, p. 69) to apply to the social, political, or economic constraints that slow or suppress the impact of new technological advancements in a culture. In Composition's culture, whether related to the teaching of writing through the use of computers or to assessment procedures, the law of suppression of radical potential exits for the classic reasons that Winston outlined.

Needs of Institutions

There must exist an opportunity and a motivating reason for an institution to adopt new technologies. Innovation in computer-enhanced composition or in writing assessment will not be accepted widely or solely on its merits. The institution has to see a clear social, political, or economic benefit to develop innovative technologies.

Some institutions, George Mason University among others, have set mandates for computer technology use. Clearly, colleges and universities see a need for assessment, particularly outcomes-based education programs, because of state legislative orders or accreditation requirements regarding accountability in university learning. At the K–12 level, the state and federal governments have mandated districts to include both technologies in the curricula, and school districts must conform to specific models of accountability to stay within "safe ranges" and avoid governmental takeovers.

Accountability, which can be defined in any number of ways—from student retention to course work achievement to whether acts of student violence are reported—becomes tied to institutional support at the legislative levels. Colleges and universities see this with the required campus violence reports published each year, just as school districts see their violence reports published annually along with their school test scores. It is conceivable that federal legislation may push for university graduation rates to be published, similarly to the NCAA graduation and retention rates that are made public each year.

Therefore, a need exists to continue funding for accountability. Including computer technology in the higher education curriculum becomes an institutional need because of the social pressures exerted by prospective and incoming students (and their parents), who believe this is an integral part of learning in the 21st century. The social pressures also come from area businesses and industries that desire highly trained workers to perform on the job. To compete with nearby colleges and universities for students, each institution sees the need to invest some money into computer infrastructure and upkeep. Again, a need to compete exists. If Composition is to move forward substantially in its technological convergence and achieve real radical potential in writing evaluation, then teachers and scholars in the field have to demonstrate there is some genuine institutional need for this to happen. Writing programs have to show how the institution can fulfill these needs that arise from social pressures and competition and be accountable to the various stakeholders connected to the campus.

Other Technologies' Requirements

Advancements in current technologies related to the teaching of writing also have to indicate that there is an opportunity to make a change in how evaluation and instruction are handled. For better or worse, writing instructors are witnessing the entrance of computerized essay grading, as in the growing use of ETS' E-Rater and Criterion systems as well as the highly publicized Intelligent Essay Assessor. This shift illustrates a change in the way writing assessment is conducted. Consequently, those faculty members interested in cultivating a different pedagogical focus using computers and assessment technologies must show others in the institution how the transformation will benefit them socially, politically, or economically. As I noted in chapter 4, programs like the Online Learning Record and TOPIC/ICON are fledgling models of deep assessment. Until such time that more widespread recognition of these online assessment models occurs, sound-bite projects like E-Rater and the Intelligent Essay Assessor will continue to receive great attention in the media and from administrations. This is because the underlying concepts of the latter programs meld computers and writing assessment in directions that institutional heads view as being beneficial politically and economically (the machine can efficiently score more essays per hour compared with a reader, thus saving costs and showing accountability to various stakeholders). Likewise, the media will always hop on stories along these lines because this blending of technologies illustrates shifts in education, which in the current social climate tends to garner newsworthiness.

Regulations and Legal Actions

If the technological transformations cause sudden shifts in the status quo, suggested Winston (1998), we should expect to see the occurrence of rising political clout and legal or governmental actions as a backlash. Clearly, with the Communications Decency Act of 1996, the U.S. Patriot Act of 2002 and the U.S. Patriot Act II, and other attempts at Internet-curbing legislation, this backlash is happening. Similarly with assessment there is an equal political and governmental push to move "back to basics" and focus on standardized skill- and-drill testing or normed writing exams. The growing number of K–12 challenges to the No Child Left Behind Act now occurring across the country illustrates the difficulties such forms of accountability have in an era of technological convergence.

This legislative backlash happens even though educators at all grade levels generally promote authentic assessment practices in the classroom that account for disparities in students' learning. The CUNY assessment troubles in 1998 reflect this concern at the college level, for example. The SUNY assessment program passed in 2004 also underscores legislative backlash in higher education. In these instances where political clout is wielded to ensure that accountability is met, the law of suppressing radical potential can be enacted to withhold funding or faculty lines, to reallocate faculty, or to deny tenure or promotion to faculty who do not conform to political influence linked to either technological form. We only have to look closely at how No Child Left Behind is applied to school districts to see the problems higher education faces should similar accountability legislation be proposed for college level learning. "Failing" K–12 schools under the No Child Left Behind Act can be taken over by the government or its agent, students can transfer to other local schools if room exists in the nearby school, or schools can close. Listing these bleak options is not designed as an appeal to fear as to what might happen should state and federal legislation related to accountability extend to higher education. My purpose in showing the effects of No Child Left Behind at the K–12 level is to offer a cautionary tale as to what happens when there is a significant shift in the status quo regarding technology and society. It is clearly important for university writing instructors to have an awareness of No Child Left Behind and its effects, because our students are coming out of schools that must follow the letter of the Act.

Current General Social Forces

Increasing popularity or public opinion supporting technological transformation produces a social climate where changes are welcomed. However, if change disrupts the status quo—and generally, a significant technological change is disruptive—then fiscal constraints, political enthusiasm, and social skepticism arise. This is easily observed in the popular media. Stories abound in the daily papers and television reports regarding how computers enhance student learning and how industry needs workers trained in computer use. Even the online magazine *Salon* (1999) has displayed an interest in the computer essay grading process, as did the defunct academic-based monthly, *Lingua Franca* (1999). Simultaneously, nationally syndicated columnists and local or wire reporters disparage the Internet and computer use (as in the "too much online computer time leads to depression" scare that grabbed Philadelphia's media in 1999). Likewise, assessment faces the same fate. Most local or regional papers run education beat stories on how their schools did in statewide assessment exams, which begets parental sighs of relief or shouts of anger for "more computers, less X" or "more X, fewer computers" depending on the results of their school district's assessment. The national news media also pick up on these stories and elevate them. For instance, in January 1999, *Time* ran a cover feature on the connection between children doing too much homework to assessment results. The conclusion: Kids do too much homework, and school-wide assessment is ranked higher than the students' daily achievements.

Although the K–12 schools face the brunt of most of these reports, colleges and their administrators are not immune to them. Yearly the "students can't write well" phenomenon trickles into the university system through the national media's punditry and sets up compositionists for a fall. In January 2003, the *Chronicle of Higher Education* took aim on this topic. Students who have suffered years of educational neglect in their literacy skills because of the "teaching to the test method" are expected to have those problems erased within 15 weeks of entering a college or university in addition to learning current techniques in computer and information literacy. Those students who cannot erase their deficiencies in writing while grasping computer usage, and there are substantial numbers who do not master both areas in their first semester, are unfairly tagged in the media by reporters or columnists bearing a strong political agenda. These students are then frequently used at many institutions as the reasons for suppressing the potential for changing curriculum, especially when money is involved. The bad press surrounding this situation pushes local institutions' administrators to check up on their writing faculty to see how their university measures up compared with what George Will, John Leo, Sven Birkerts, Lynne Cheyney, or some other columnist wrote.

Arguably, this practice is not fair to the students nor is it fair to the instructors. But knowing that the law of suppressed radical potential is at work in these situations helps to explain why writing program administrators and their faculties receive mandates and charges that run counter to each other as well as orders that other academic programs do not. As Brian Winston (1998) eloquently argued, social, economic, and political forces are three "supervening social necessities" that both accelerate and decelerate technological advancement (p. 69). The media, as a strong shaper for public opinion, send all of us mixed accounts regarding the competing classroom technologies of computers and assessment. In turn, administrations send mixed messages to departments and faculties regarding computer and assessment technologies, as the social, economic, and political messages waver on a regular basis. Consequently, writing instructors are caught between accelerating and decelerating technological use in the classroom depending on the cultural tide.

Recognizing that the law of suppressed radical potential functions wherever technology surfaces in a culture is important for understanding how writing instructors can develop assessment practices that align with the shifting demands for technology in the classroom. The convergence process between these two technologies in Composition will be fraught with moments of acceleration and periods of delay until the needs of the institution, social forces, and, unfortunately, legislative and regulatory effects are met and some kind of stabilizing environment occurs. The best news is that stabilization does eventually happen with all technologies. However, no one can predict when this stability emerges. Currently, computer technology is moving far faster than assessment technology, and compositionists have the ability to advance the students' writing processes much more quickly using vastly complex genres and hardware or software combinations compared with what the standard evaluation methodologies can accommodate. The result is that many faculty and programs are hindered in their hopes to upgrade computer networks or systems because of the economic aspects of technology. Simultaneously, faculty and programs are constrained by the social and political pressures that drive the need for outdated assessment methods that evaluate writing in networked environments.

These realizations led me to recognize that the traditional writing assessment practices so common to my department and to other programs are usually inappropriate for the activities that take place in Room 25 or in similar rooms at other universities. Nor do I think these traditional writing assessment practices function well for the types of writing students in grades K–12 need to learn to succeed in college and in the workforce (see Hillocks, 2002, for an in-depth of four state K–12 writing assessments). However, these older writing assessment trends correspond nicely to what the punditry support and the public think measures good writing. Students' mechanical skills are not necessarily in question with networked writing as they are with pen-and-paper texts, as HTML writing requires strong syntactic skills for a web page to load properly. The same goes for writing in MOOspace or in the blogosphere—poor syntax leads to an inability to perform. Most instructors find that students whose punctuation or spelling skills are weak have great difficulties with even the simplest Internet search. This "problem" forces students to check their work more carefully, enlist the help of others nearby when something is not working correctly, or discuss their problems running a search engine or HTML code with the instructor before moving on to future activities. These are not necessarily bad things in a collaborative writing classroom.

Equally important is that I learned many aspects of a hot technology like assessment have possibilities for being incorporated into a cool medium in the writing classroom. Rather than heating up the assessment process, the coolness of the computer medium offers the opportunity to account for the originality that students frequently display in identifying the writing practices or strategies needed to produce a response.

However, given the oppositional qualities of a hot technology like assessment and a cool one like computers, finding practices that work in one system as well as the other can be troublesome, especially in classroom situations where outcomes-based education is instituted. Still, I learned that it is indeed possible to meld the two technologies to create an assessment for adequacy. Although traditional assessment structures such as rigid rubrics regularly address surface concerns, performance assessment tends to be a more instinctive approach for the complex tasks and real audiences that materialize in a computer-enhanced classroom. In current practice, though, many performance assessment contexts either are limited in their scope or are too highly structured to be of much value in a fluid environment like cyberspace. Extended performance assessments, like writing instructors can find in the Online Learning Record or TOPIC/ICON, lean toward open, broadly defined, problem-solving and communication-infused activities that occur in networked writing. However, a significant difficulty with performance assessment is that the current dominant perspective in educational tests and measurements is to use performance assessment as a support for traditional methods (Gronlund, 1998) rather than a stand-alone method for measuring student achievement. Some test and measurement proponents, suggested Norman Gronlund (1998), view performance assessment as being too relative, too easily given without clear criteria to be of use in either evaluation or grading settings. According to test-and-measurement traditionalists, the results of performance assessments for evaluation or grading tend to distort student achievement or effort (Gronlund, 1998). This position needs to be weighed against offering an assessment plan that speaks to a wide range of integrated online writing activities.

A second challenge regarding the use of performance assessment as it is generally conducted is that all too often the evaluation still centers on the product even though the measurement addresses students' process. In my own classes I have found that by only focusing assessment on the students' products and not on their processes, four situations repeatedly arise.

The Finished Product Does Not Function in the Ways a Student Expects

This scenario happens when students do not understand the procedures needed to upload graphics, establish links, or send posts to lists. Frequently the disconnect between function and expectation occurs because students are aiming for the grade outcome and not the experience of learning how to create and writing in electronic space. These individuals will jump ahead in the work, skip important early steps, or want to compare a new program with something they have at home or in the dorm. In this situation, early assessment that centers on the processes involved with setting up various e-texts intervenes with students' developing "bad habits" that affect their later success in creating those electronic texts on their own. Performance assessment can range from F2F discussions with students as they sit at a terminal to periodic e-mail reviews of student sites during the brainstorming or writing process. Students can also be encouraged to post questions and problems about their work to a class discussion list to have their peers offer suggestions for improvement.

Students Have No Clear Idea Why Their Electronic Text Fails To Communicate Effectively

With a performance model that focuses on the various stages of production and includes student reflection at each step, students consider what qualities of each electronic genre are identified as being important or effective in reaching a real audience. Performance assessment that only centers on the finished product allows students to forget what they have done at each level, so many are unaware of the overall impression their e-text has on an audience.

Inauthentic Assessment Is Created by Instructors Only Assessing The Product

E-texts should be considered as works in progress and need to be measured accordingly. Writers tinker with their web sites and list moderators tend to the mechanics of their discussion lists on a regular basis. Hypertext authors revise links or add new ones. Not accounting for past and present revisions student writers make to their e-texts is unrealistic in measuring a writer's growth. A semester's time constraints already place a serious restriction on the students' abilities to construct, revise, append, and submit electronic work for a grade. Time is further constrained if the class is on quarter-term. Some e-texts require writers to return again and again to shape the finished product. Some e-texts, like MOOs, blogs, or highly interactive web sites, may never be truly finished. Although a final evaluation is inevitable, and grading on promise or potential is risky, instructors can use deep assessment to measure students' progress to date. Compositionists can examine the archives to see how students' works have evolved over the term and evaluate based on a body of data, not just a single project.

A Full Range of Electronic Writing Is Rarely Included in the Assessment

Unfortunately, when many students submit their e-portfolios, writing instructors only see the completed work and not all the revisions that happen. Also, most electronic portfolios reflect essayistic writing. This privileges standard academic writing genres and alphabetic literacy over more mundane texts that commonly appear in electronic communication. Missing in most e-portfolios are the e-mail exchanges, the list messages, and the conference postings, all of which are important traces of how students' finished pieces evolve over a term. From these conversations and fragments, faculty can decide whether the work is the student's own, whether students mastered certain tasks or relied heavily on the kindness of others who had already acquired important techniques or strategies in visual rhetoric or electronic communication. Including archival data in the assessment also helps build reflective teaching practices, because instructors can trace whether a project had merit for the students.

Over the last few years, I have come to realize how assessment technology must change to accommodate this newer computer technology in the writing classroom. Instead of discovering ways of capturing students' curiosity to begin writing with computers, as I had to 5 or 10 years ago, now my emphasis is on motivating students' concerns for what is at stake when they create a web site, post certain types of e-mail messages, or construct a hypertext story or poem. This shift in my focus has not always been easy to make, but I believe it has made me a better teacher of writing.

HOT AND COOL TECHNOLOGIES CONVERGE IN THE WRITING FROM ROOM 25

Room 25 can be a colorful and active place. The classroom pace runs from silent tapping of keys to the frenetic sounds of students on deadline, depending on the time of the semester and the pressures of looming assignments. Although each of my classes spend some time throughout the semester in Room 25, the classes I teach completely computer enhanced are my undergraduate Writing, Research, and Technology class, and my graduate-level Writing for Electronic Communities and Information Architecture classes. These three classes are the ones that taught me more about what it means to question writing assessment in the age of technological convergence. Each of these classes made me realize that writing assessment is frequently a teacher-referenced experience even though it is couched in the language of student-centeredness. The instructor always undergoes performance assessment in a writing class; the students' collective ability to react competently under specific conditions measures the instructor's performance.

In Room 25, though, the group dynamic changes to something almost Zen-like. Even though I am still the instructor of record, the professor, the students make the courses their own. I am teaching, but I am not teaching. I am assessing, but I am not assessing. As students work with various programs and texts, the class begins to self-assess their efforts more thoroughly than one might first expect. Sometimes their judgments are made supportively, sometimes teasingly, but their comments are always insightful in that they focus solely on how the e-text is or could be received by an audience. In this process, validation does not come from me. Confirmation of each student's ability comes from those who sign up for discussion lists or blogs that the students create, from the clients who received web sites designed by students for a final assignment, from the MOOs students enter for the first time, or from class members who struggled with course readings, blogging, or similar tasks.

I do not wish to overly romanticize the writing that occurs in Room 25. Michael Joyce wrote that electronic texts are "belief structures" (2001, p. 17) in that people are "apt to believe that even the most awkward contemporary technology of literacy embodies the associational schema of the texts that it presents" (2001, p. 18). Teaching in computer-enhanced writing courses echoes Joyce's thoughts on belief structures. Sometimes instructors are quick to believe that even the most inelegant or commonplace student e-text embodies the associational schema of the other texts it presents. There are hundreds, if not thousands, of student-produced electronic texts that succeed (but probably should not) because of the belief structures coupled with what exists on screen. Many of my students have produced these e-texts, and probably most veteran writing instructors can name a half-dozen or so student e-texts that succeeded because of a presumed belief that the work carried far more associational schema than it truly did. This is why deep assessment is needed in the computer-enhanced writing class. Writing instructors need to meld hot and cool technologies to challenge our belief structures about students' e-texts, just as we push our students to confront their own belief structures as they create these texts.

The convergence of hot and cool technologies in Room 25 has led me to want to construct *desire paths* for computer-enhanced writing assessment. When I wrote my dissertation, I spent long hours studying contemporary architecture to understand the connections architectural processes have to writing (Penrod, 1994). What fascinated me was how users of an architectural space frequently create preferred paths that do not always follow the prescribed pavement. Desire paths lead us toward reaching our goals or direction on our own terms. As we set that path, we look carefully at and for obstacles as well as continuity to direct us. A desire path for technological convergence suggests that evaluation is as much of a journey as the processes connected to writing an e-text.

More pragmatically, desire paths for assessing e-texts are grounded in the traces and details that offer helpful statements that such-and-so genuinely exists, regardless of whether that characteristic is positive or negative or whether the writer's purpose is to inform or to entertain. The following desire paths emerged as I evaluated the writing produced in Room 25:

- My comments continually arose from direct learning situations to provide feedback that motivated students to improve their efforts. Students solicited more of my comments earlier in the process to help them learn how to conduct self-assessment as the courses progressed. Students understood where they were in the course without constant reference to grades.
- There are always volumes of information to draw on to illuminate points or to address concerns. Consequently, I find myself working harder to improve the quality of my instruction to facilitate student learning.
- My assessment processes are completely integrated with my instruction. The students' evaluations originate wholly from their online written work, which is visible to all. To gain outside perspectives, some classes adopted the exhibition model to show their sites to friends, colleagues, and family during the construction phases. All other aspects of the students' writing for the semester, from the list discussions to the MOO and web site projects, were entirely classroom generated and archived. Archiving the work meant I could trace each student's progress carefully.
- A rich variety of data from which to evaluate students' learning developed and was easily accessible to anyone who asked.
- As classes progress, students are asked to collaborate on changes to correct any real or perceived deficiencies in the courses. Involving students in the modification of a computer-enhanced class helped establish positive cooperation between students and the instructor and promoted assessment reform.
- The curriculum became more pliable within the boundaries of the course proposals to respond to different student abilities and comfort levels with technology.

The last desire path was filled with obstacles. Conducting deep and continuous writing assessment is time consuming, sometimes mentally draining, and often physically exhausting for my eyes. Something else happened while this path was under construction, though. I truly enjoyed every moment with these students, watching them work through assorted design problems, technical considerations, and media selections. As they sought my comments during the stages of producing an assignment, assessment became an easy give-and-take between writers and readers. The class initiated and responded to questions of visual rhetoric or written rhetoric, as I regularly made available one or two of the class members' projects to critique. Evaluation became an ongoing part of the course, not just an add-on at the end of the semester. The desire path for melding hot and cool technologies in Room 25, while obstacle filled on some days, was forming.

The students and I no longer saw ourselves as students and professor as we journeyed down this path. Instead, we were designers and writers who collaborated on various projects. The divisiveness surrounding responding and grading assignments seemed less so. When I put forward comments, suggestions, and a grade for an assignment, students did not have the usual sense of detachment that comes from their being disappointed by not receiving an expected grade. Rather, students paid attention to my comments and suggestions to improve and they tinkered with their projects to reflect those changes they thought were worthwhile. The individual grades became less an object inflicted on the class and more a benchmark from which students could develop future revisions. My grading hand feels lighter than it has in years.

Traveling down this desire path in writing assessment taught me that annexing hot and cool technologies adds complex layers of stylistic and rhetorical reasoning, decision making, and language use as well as technical ability that highlight student proficiencies, weaknesses, and literacies in a profound way. The coolness of computer technology mediates the heat of writing assessment practices that require instructors to guess at the proficiency of middle-range students. And the computer's distancing effect combined with visual elements in electronic texts reduces the possibilities of having me fall under the spell of those writers who are facile with language but who labor with ideas or techne.

Grading also became a much easier process for me in Room 25. Because of the established audit trail, the continual interaction with students as they worked in various electronic genres, and the contributions students made to the direction of the class, I came to know each of these students and their work very well. I understood where an individual student's electronic writing excelled and where it was in need of improvement. The archives that emerged for deep assessment allowed me to pore over earlier files and watch student growth occur in stages during the semester.

Grading became clearer for students too, because my comments were always couched in the context of what led to the final submission and reflected both my attitudes and responses to their work as well as the student's own attitudes and responses. Even though the semester created artificial end points where grades must be given, the students realized that networked writing truly is a work in progress. As I wrote this chapter, nearly 3 years after I first began teaching in Room 25, I received two e-mails, one from Doretta and one from Kamau, telling me they are still working on the web sites created for one of my classes. Both said they were tweaking and refining different parts of their sites. Then they warned me that they would be looking for me on campus soon to get feedback on their improved sites. Other students too have contacted me over the last few years, telling me that they are now creating web sites for employers or on a freelance basis. In their postings, these students always begin with something like, "I'll bet you never figured I'd keep doing web pages after your class, but guess what" (Wendy, personal correspondence, October 2001).

Needless to say, the e-mails I receive from former students astound me. I do not remember the last time students writing in a papertext format sent me a message a few years later telling me they are revising their work and asking me for a critique. This experience has made me think that convergence may indeed provide a real renaissance for writing instruction in the years ahead.

What I relearned about hot and cool technologies by teaching in Room 25 is that instructors can use these technologies to create inclusive activities that bring together students and instructors under a common purpose: to discover how writing can be a communicative act. The coolness of computer technology mediates the direct heat of evaluation, as both students and professors are pressed continually to communicate with each other in electronic environments. Reducing assessment's heat allowed me to refocus on what makes student evaluation successful for the teacher and the students. Student evaluation works when it is immediate, when it is directed at the work, and when students have a chance to revise to make their work stronger. This rediscovery helped me to center my efforts to meet those aims.

Teaching in Room 25 showed me that inclusive, effective assessment requires instructors to take risks with their authority, with their time, and with their students. Effective assessment in electronic environments also asks instructors to undertake new courses of action to respond to networked writing and the corresponding e-texts that come out of the course work. My grading hand rests even more easily on the mouse pad now; I am not so quick to overwrite or override students' ideas as I was a few years ago. Although I still intervene sometimes when a student asks for specific technical advice, my approach to teaching writing now comes through questioning and observing patterns that relate to the interaction between a student's visual and verbal rhetoric rather than through overt correction and rewriting of documents. And, even better, my grading hand does not want to overwrite web sites or other hypertext documents. These days, my comments are sent by e-mail directly to the student, or if we are in class, I am sitting next to the student discussing her work and she manipulates the mouse to make the changes she wants.

Relearning assessment from my experiences in Room 25 has made me more aware of what some students undergo in the evaluation process. The heat generated by traditional writing assessment practices is sometimes more than what these students can stand. For some students, the heat is so intense, it shuts down their ability to write anything, anywhere, at any time, and in any medium. The computer's coolness takes some of the heat away for certain students. In the process of ludic writing, the act of composing becomes play and it makes writing less stressful in short bursts.

Still, it is not always easy to show people how melding these two technologies can be an exciting pedagogical opportunity. The prospects seem particularly small when there are limitations or inconveniences attached to the technologies (e.g., system problems, software glitches, the lack of an established or normed evaluation rubric, etc.) or when a group is wedded to a particular communication domain, such as print documentation. Layer these moments with striving to find compatible assessment procedures to mesh with networked writing beyond the superficial models offered by

ETS, Vantage, WebCT, NiceNet, Blackboard, and others, and it becomes understandable why many faculty feel constrained in blending these two technologies in the networked classroom.

However, when enough familiarity with hot and cool technologies is built up within a program, a campus, or a cultural system like Composition, then the law of suppressed radical potential no longer applies and the changes brought about by convergence multiply—quickly. Some may ask how long this familiarity-building process takes. Unfortunately, this is a highly localized evolution. The worst-case scenario for building bridges of familiarity in a culture comes from Johann Gutenberg, whose printing press needed 150 years before it churned out what we recognize as being a book or a periodical (Fidler, 1997, p. 16). That is five times the 30-year rule outlined by Paul Saffo.

One hopes that most faculty members and administrators grasp these ideas in a much shorter time than did Gutenberg's followers. In 3 years, I relearned that linking writing assessment technologies with computer-based composition can lead to some very powerful student learning about language and rhetoric. In 6 years, I learned how to train my grading hand from overwriting student work. I am hopeful that younger faculty members, especially those in graduate school now, will emerge with well-trained grading hands and minds. Based on what I discovered in Room 25 it is not unreasonable to think that within the next 5 to 10 years in Composition, authentic and deep writing assessment connected to computer-enhanced writing classes will be commonplace. As more writing instructors become familiar with and comfortable with computer and assessment technologies, and younger faculty members who have been steeped in visual rhetoric and technorhetoric throughout their lives join departments, perhaps the law of suppressed radical potential will disappear. Then, instead of having two separate hot and cool technologies, or one very lukewarm one, Composition's practitioners will have a stronger understanding of how to blend these technologies in meaningful ways. In those days that lie ahead, today's desire paths will become the well-worn, established avenues for writing instruction.

Chapter 6

Access Before Assessment?

The preceding chapters discussed a range of theoretical, political, textual, and practical issues connected to the convergence of computer technology with writing assessment in Composition. Each chapter attempted to link internetworked writing's creative methods and processes to the various factors that influence assessment in the culture of Composition. In this chapter, I turn to concerns regarding changing the university culture to make it more hospitable for Composition's convergence to take hold completely. These matters center on the idea of access and how it affects students and their writing in an age of technological convergence.

These days it seems that no one can discuss computers, assessment, or higher education without addressing access. Access is the metaphorical elephant on the table; everyone sees it, knows its presence, and offers suggestions on how to work around it, but no one can make that elephant get down from the table. Although I cannot presume to make the elephant budge in this chapter, I do hope to nudge it a bit so other writing specialists can take up the discussion and push the elephant a little closer to the edge of the table.

In her 1997 presentation to the CCCC Special Interest Group in Computers, Cynthia Selfe noted that before assessment can take place in the computer-enhanced writing classroom, students must have greater direct access to technology. This is a point on which most compositionists agree. The conflicts that exist between students' direct access to computers—particularly in their early years of schooling—and the low achievement scores on large-scale writing assessment tests like the NAEP must quickly be addressed in the age of convergence. The 1998 and 2000 governmental studies indicate that families whose incomes are above $40,000 per year, regardless of race, have computers or Internet capability in the home, whereas those families who are under the $40,000 mark rarely have in-home computers (NTIA, 2000). Although anecdotal evidence suggests that more students have computer access in the home, it is unclear as to whether more families under $40,000 do have computers and cable or dial-up access in the home than in the past (Alter, 1999).

According to the studies taken, this "digital divide" is evidenced most clearly in minority households, but Caucasians in the lower income groups are also becoming part of the growing "information have-nots" (NTIA, 2000). Consequently, these students' information and technological literacy levels, just like their traditional literacy levels on national and statewide assessment tests, appear to have their roots in the family's socioeconomic conditions. Clearly, computer access—like fair access to writing assessment—is a class issue just as much as it is a racial issue. Computers, reading materials, pens, pencils, books, magazines, newspapers, and paper cost money that some families do not have. And it is not a question of whether students can use the local library for some of these items. In many communities throughout the United States, libraries are regionally located, and poor or working-class families outside of America's urban centers may not have the transportation or the time to get children to libraries on a regular basis. With the cutbacks in local governments, items like bookmobiles that could travel to the children are drastically reduced, if not eliminated, in some parts of the country. Those who can take their children to libraries have to face the reality that many public libraries are eliminating hours, staff, and equipment to meet budgetary shortfalls. These issues make public library usage difficult for a significant segment of America's youngsters. Without some type of public support for technology and information literacy, it is highly plausible that there will be a growing gap in many students' skills, at least in the next few decades to come.

Without all students having better access to technology in the writing curriculum, any sort of ongoing, online writing assessment is going to be haphazard at best. Certainly, without language arts and composition teachers being better trained in the use of technology, any future writing assessment plans will most likely follow along the lines of current–traditional forms that focus solely on grammar, mechanics, and official modes of discourse.

In a just, fair, and equitable educational structure, writing assessment would wait until every student is sufficiently wired to computers and instructors were well-trained in the ways of presenting writing through technology. But the K–college educational structure is not just, fair, and equitable. At the university level, it is especially inhospitable to the humanities in general and Composition in particular. This wave of hostility continues as long as a corporate mindset permeates university missions and philosophies. Danling Fu, writing in Sunstein and Lovell's collection, *The Portfolio Standard* (2000), observed, "Education suffers because, like this country, it is caught between two value systems: the democratic, human values system and the economic, marketing values system" (p. 114). Most who teach in writing or in the humanities would argue that the nation's colleges and universities are leaning more toward the economic, marketing values system in higher education. This trend directly affects the blending of computers and writing assessment at the university.

One only has to peruse articles in *The Atlantic Monthly* like "The Kept University" by Eyal Press and Jennifer Washburn (March 2000) to recognize that what Cynthia Selfe argued for in her 1997 presentation probably won't happen in the near future. Press and Washburn (2000) reported that George Mason University (GMU), a state-funded university in Virginia, tightened its bonds between campus and corporation to support the region's high-tech industry. According to Press and Washburn's story, Virginia Governor James S. Gilmore promised to increase GMU's state funding up to $25 million per year provided GMU strengthened its connections to northern Virginia's growing high-tech businesses (2000, pp. 39–54). In response, GMU's president, Alan Merten, announced, "We must accept that we have a new mandate, and a new reason for [universities] being in existence .... The mandate is to be networked" (Press & Washburn, 2000, p. 51, brackets mine).

Part of Merten's mandate included that all students were to be "trained to pass a 'technology literacy' test" (Press & Washburn, 2000, p. 51). Presumably, GMU's technology literacy test would be administered by the campus' computer and information technology department, as Merten eliminated several degree programs in the humanities to accommodate this new university mandate. This cutting of programs occurred even though 1,700 students signed a petition of protest and 180 professors in GMU's College of Arts and

Sciences sent a letter arguing that humanities education does prepare students beyond "technological proficiency" (Press & Washburn, 2000, p. 51). Although the GMU response is probably an accurate reflection of how those of us in the humanities think, Merten's rejoinder summarizes the turn administrative and legislative bodies have made toward higher education.

President Merten's defense of his slashing programs reflects the corporate mindset infused in the language of higher education and the "market-model university" (Engell & Dangerfield, 1998):

> There was a time when universites weren't held accountable for much— people just threw money at them .... People with money are more likely to give you money if you have restructured and repositioned yourself, got rid of stuff that you don't need to have. They take a very dim view of giving you money to run an inefficient organization .... We have a commitment to produce people who are employable in today's technology work force. (Press & Washburn. 2000, p. 51)

It seems unimaginable to anyone in Composition to think that writing, reading, and thinking would make people less employable in the Information Age. If anything, writing, reading, and thinking should make students more employable. However, compositionists can see with increasing regularity that state universities, especially smaller state universities vying for budget dollars with larger research universities, clearly follow principles similar to George Mason University's. Each year, more state governments are slashing funding for higher education, and with these cuts comes the reduction of departmental support for humanities programs. To offset these cuts, state governments offer money to their universities to create curricula or programs that "sell." In the market-model university, courses or programs that generate money, develop venture money, or lure money in for the University have priority over all others (Engell & Dangerfield, 1998). These courses are the ones students have access to.

Composition, as it is currently configured at most institutions, does not generate money, develop venture money, or lure money in for the university. Composition mostly prepares large numbers of incoming and transfer students for work in other majors across campus. In retail terms, Composition is a "loss leader" for universities. Writing specialists only have to look at how literacy, especially information literacy, is assessed in the market-model university to see the dark side of convergence and to realize that the humanities have a very important role to play in developing students' reading and writing ability in this new era.

In Engell and Dangerfield's market-model university structure (1998), technology literacy becomes reduced to sets of discrete skills, easily testable and tested throughout the students' academic career. In this framework, writing is also condensed to sets of discrete sills that can be tested and retested quite easily. In both instances, the critical aspects and nuances related to a student forming full literacy are absent. Instead, the focus is on efficiency and accountability in transmitting information. In this model, Composition could easily return to the bad old days of indirect assessment, as the market-model university format puts in place mechanisms to chop away at general education loss leaders like writing classes. Market demand drives what courses are offered, what majors are cut, and what ones are funded (Engell & Dangerfield, 1998). Because composition is a required general education course, often referred to as a "service" course, the demand for composition classes comes from the institution requiring them, and not necessarily from the current student interest in the course content. Many times, students do not appreciate the importance or value in their first-year composition sequence until later in their studies or after graduation (Light, 1999). Consequently, it becomes critical for writing specialists and program administrators to examine their programs and promote those values, benefits, and advantages that the writing sequence has at their institutions. In this discussion, it is vitally important for writing programs to "pay attention" (Selfe, 1999, p. xix) to the place electronic writing has in first-year composition, because this could be the next wave of "service learning" in colleges and universities.

In the market-model university, access is something more than students being offered opportunities to learn with computer-enhanced writing classes, as Selfe outlined (1999); access has to include what has been traditionally considered part of the American university's mission: to reason, read, and write critically. The point to access in the age of technological convergence is not to privilege one side over another in students' learning experiences; the point is to integrate all sides of reasoning, reading, and writing in a text.

To create the type of environment Selfe (1999) spoke of, where students have greater direct access to technology in the writing classroom before compositionists assess their work, requires a massive shift in the culture of higher education. Selfe's learning environment (1999) asks all of us in Composition to reimagine the teaching of writing, the assessment process, and the place of both in the university structure given the philosophical climate of fast capitalism found at most institution. However, this transformation must extend beyond the writing program.

Although it is important for agents of cultural change to come first from writing programs if the field of Composition Studies is to defend student access to both writing instruction and accurate assessment procedures that include real writing using computer technology in the university hierarchy, these individuals cannot respond to the problems in the usual ways. This is a crucial point, because computer technology has shown composition studies that the contexts in which we have "done" schooling in the past have changed. The computer has modified the relationships writing instructors have with their students and with texts. Likewise, the computer has altered the philosophies professors develop about learning, teaching, and the level of activity needed in evaluating writing. These are the areas compositionists have to build on more carefully and more forcefully to show others across campus, particularly administrators and legislators, why college writing instruction is still meaningful in a market-driven university structure.

TRANSFORMING ACCESS IN COMPOSITION

To transform access across Composition's culture, it is crucial to move to alternative ways for seeking change. Writing faculties need to ask themselves, What are the preexisting attitudes, perspectives, beliefs, and understandings the field has regarding the notion of access? This includes not just access regarding how students and faculty can engage with technology, but access related to whose voice is heard in the writing classroom, in evaluation settings, and in decisions where computers are chosen and assessment plans are made? Then, these same instructors must ask themselves the same things in relation to their own institutions. How do these dual histories affect instructors' and writing program administrators' interpretations of what takes place (or should take place) in the classroom? How will these answers influence the outcomes of the students' and instructors' learning and teaching experiences in the first-year sequence? Equally important is the question, What types of learning in the computer-enhanced writing classroom can be applied to the students' involvement in the "real world" and what are the best ways of measuring that learning? Questions like these begin constructing the philosophical and practical implications for more and better access in the college writing classroom and for future assessment methods.

Compositionists must also consider their own views on technology and whether their attitudes reflect an "instrumental or substantive" (Feenberg, 1991) position. That is, do we see technology, in either assessment or computer form, as a value-neutral tool that conforms to the needs of various writing purposes? Or do we see these two technologies as another type of social system that reorganizes the entire social world in our classrooms? Again, the answers we ourselves put forward, and those solutions our programs or departments establish, offer important insights into the implications for the types of access we desire in the college writing class. How we answer these questions also will reflect how we come to assess the types of writing produced in networked settings.

As a discipline, Composition should be speaking louder in recognizing the importance of establishing and fostering multiple literacies in our students to meet the demands of writing various e-texts. Using the body of works produced by numerous scholars, researchers, and teachers in the field, Composition needs to do better in its investigation of what the pragmatic goals and rationales are for incorporating these numerous abilities into the various levels of college writing that now exist. There has to be greater discussion of when and where, pedagogically, these computer-enhanced writing activities can and should be incorporated into the entire writing sequence. For instance, what are suitable online writing activities for basic writers or ESL students—do these instructors focus on chat and lists to build fluency, or should they set up some sort of interactive writing environment on DIWE or WebCT, BlackBoard, or others? Would e-journal writing or blogging be better activities? Or should these instructors create something more challenging for ESL students, like a MOO?

Actually, when in the composition sequences should students MOO or blog? Is entering MOO or blog space part of first-year comp, advanced composition, professional writing, or graduate study? At what point in the students' composing experience does visual rhetoric enter—or should it enter? Even though each institution has unique needs and interests connected to its student population and various limits on its ability to use technology, the sharing of ideas related to these e-textual topics is important. Wider discussions like these help newcomers or skeptics better understand how the technologies interact in the classroom and show them that a universalized computers and writing assessment program appears impossible to carry out.

Faculty who have knowledge of both technologies are necessary to begin the discussions and to guide their institutions and programs to find those options that work best for them, and not what was just announced in the media that is happening at a large research university, an Ivy, or a small liberal arts college. Writing specialists can carve out a new language to discuss these intersecting technologies, one that melds terms from computer-enhanced composition practices and from writing assessment in particular ways that speak about how to best evaluate students' growth when they are engaging in internetworked writing. At most institutions, compositionists can and should take the lead in offering best practices in converging these two technologies.

Perhaps, though, these individuals' greatest benefit to their programs and to Composition is that they can articulate the different social and cultural values that dwell within both technologies and how student learning is affected. Compositionists who understand both computers and writing assessment can help negotiate how students can be creative when their learning outcomes are increasingly being driven by narrowing local, state, and national standards.

HOW SHOULD ACCESS BE INCREASED BEFORE WE ASSESS?

Writing specialists need to consider two elements to the notion of access—a way for students and instructors to approach or enter these technologies as well as the right or opportunity for students and instructors to use these technologies. Far too often, Composition's culture focuses on the latter view and forgets the former. Unless both aspects of the discussion are taken into account simultaneously, the entire concept of access is meaningless. For the two technologies to work in tandem in the composition classroom, there needs to be an equal and mutual understanding of how students and instructors can move toward using these technologies. Then it seems the opportunities can emerge for both instructors and students to use the technologies in meaningful, beneficial ways in the writing classroom.

Companies like WebCT, BlackBoard, SCT, ETS, Nuventive, and others recognize this point. As Batson (2002) reported, these technology vendors have or are preparing e-portfolio tools to work with their programs (p. 15). Individual instructors and program directors like Fred Kemp (2002) realize this point, too, because Kemp's TOPIC/ICON software represents a different method for students and instructors to approach networked writing and assessment. However, there need to be many more choices available for faculty. Not every instructor wants to be saddled with "course-in-a-box" software that limits her instructional options. Many will find that the ETS Criterion software merely replicates the usual holistic scoring approach to papers that ETS has done for decades, even though Criterion offers checklists and feedback to writers as well as stores the data in "portfolio" form. Nor does every program have the need or the bandwidth available to borrow or adapt an intensive system like TOPIC/ICON. Developing full access to both technologies means the field of Composition Studies should have a range of database choices so instructors and programs can select what works best for their needs. Full access does not mean depending on one vendor because that's what the university purchased, nor does it mean individual instructors have to reinvent large databases to fit smaller programmatic needs.

In writing about cross-curricular design portfolios, Jeffrey D. Wilhelm wrote, "You don't create, define, or find meaning for yourself by doing someone else's work; you do it by creating and constructing meanings in actual situations that are of great personal relevance and social significance" (2000, p. 15). Wilhelm's observation should also extend to how Composition encourages access to technology before instructors assess student e-texts. Writing instructors and their programs must decide which learning situations have great personal relevance and social significance for melding these two technologies. That said, there are places within academic work loads and departmental requirements where faculties can begin exploring those actual situations that bear on personal relevance and social significance to increase technological access.

Perhaps one of the simplest ways to encourage the growth of tandem technologies is for tenure and promotion committees to consider the creation of software that offers assessment for e-texts as being akin to other scholarly activity. The fight for publication is fierce for junior faculty members; there are too few scholarly journals and presses for all the younger scholars producing papers and manuscripts to meet tenure deadlines. If writing programs supported those faculty members who are skilled with computers and writing assessment technologies to produce recognized alternative scholarship that could be published and disseminated (similar to what happens with book contracts), more options for the field would exist. These younger scholars would be producing important contributions to Composition instead of trying to reinvent the next big idea for an article or a book in traditional print settings. Their efforts would increase access to both technologies; instructors and writing programs could, over time, become familiar with the software or could test several pieces of software before making a decision. And, this can be a way for writing programs to bring money into the market-model university, because most institutions have guidelines for profit sharing if faculty use campus materials to generate for-profit items.

A second way to promote fuller access to the two technologies is to generate more cross-talk about what writing faculties expect students to know and do with computers. Computer-friendly and assessment- friendly instructors need to share their views with others on campus and in the discipline. As convergence continues, both camps must learn to teach together. One place to begin is with conversations regarding what students know and do in various computer-enhanced writing classes. Then the discussion can evolve into what instructors value in these activities. From there, a third turn emerges. That is how faculty can evaluate e-texts in a fair and equitable manner.

Another suggestion for increasing access is to construct faculty in-service workshops or retreats that focus on the best practices in computer-enhanced writing classes and how those instructors evaluate those assignments. These dialogues offer the possibility of linking conversations with artifacts, in essence, showing colleagues how the two technologies work together rather than just telling them in a presentation. Having writing specialists discover that there are many ways to conduct online assessment beyond course-in-a-box options ensures greater access to new (and possibly better) models. Compositionists who are comfortable with both technologies can serve as mentors to newcomers who wish to explore these areas in their classrooms.

One other possibility for producing more student access to technologies is to establish better ties to the K–12 teachers to exchange ideas for using both computers and assessment in the writing class. Most K–12 instructors draw their knowledge from different bases, such as education or tests and measurements. Their positions can help us see problems and challenges for technorhetoric in a different light, because college writing instructors can observe how future students progress with these technologies long before the students arrive on campus. Writing specialists can begin to understand the K–12 teachers' institutional demands placed on them by others regarding the use of rigid rubrics, skill-based instruction, and basic computer usage (i.e., word processing or PowerPoint). In turn, compositionists can offer classroom ideas that arise out of postprocess theory, "rearticulated" writing assessment (Huot, 2002), or visual rhetoric to stimulate and evaluate K–12 online writing activities. In addition, colleges could offer summer camps for young writers that focus on technology. In this setting, students' work is evaluated using new models of deep assessment. Similarly, campus writing programs can set up outreach services to local school districts in either a summer camp or semester-long workshop format to encourage K–12 instructors to adopt new technologies in their classes. Through these small steps, compositionists would be ensuring that their future students are better prepared technologically to meet the expectations of networked writing in the college classroom.

Access is so much more than stating that every student should have the ability to use computers or to be assessed fairly. These two items should be a given in Composition. A revised understanding of access depends on the field's awareness that to safeguard access to both technologies, many more options need to be made available to instructors and students. Although these four suggestions are only tiny steps in what can be done by compositionists to bring about technological access in the discipline, the ideas are concrete and workable for most programs or departments. If writing specialists are to become the agents of change Selfe (1999) argued for, then these four propositions move the field in the direction she hopes we take. Without better technological access for either computers or writing assessment, it is neither fair nor advantageous to assess student writing created in networked environments.

The growing need to protect and extend fair access to both technologies in Composition is a reaction to the darker side of the market-model university. Anne Herrington and Charles Moran (2001) warned compositionists of the dangers ahead if a human presence is lost in the convergence between computers and assessment. Writing, whether in electronic or print forms, should never be considered more than a mere demonstration of artful placement of words and phrases. Writing is a communicative act, dependent on situations, readers, and writers. At times, writing is efficient but it can also be ornate, foolish, playful, or abstruse. This is something writing specialists should recognize and remember, because the current software evaluation tools do not. As Herrington and Moran (2001) noted, a student's writing on the machine is far different from a student's writing to the machine. If Composition's convergence is to be a bold, new stage in its progression as a discipline, then instructors need to discover ways on their campuses to take those first incremental steps in ensuring genuine access to both technologies. To do nothing virtually guarantees a return of the heat from indirect assessment in the guise of cool technology.

CREATING ETHICAL ACCESS TO NETWORKED ENVIRONMENTS FOR ESTABLISHING ETHICAL ASSESSMENT PRACTICES

In the access battle, writing specialists must also carve out ethical spaces for networked environments in order to establish ethical assessment practices. At the heart of establishing ethical access for assessment procedures is whether instructors are teaching and measuring something important in the curriculum. In general, Composition as a discipline professes that for people to participate fully in contemporary democratic societies, computer and information literacy is almost mandatory. If this is so, in internetworked writing classes, instructors need to consider the human relationships that technology forms or shapes. For instance, how is power constructed or shared in cyberclassrooms? Which courses get to use the computers most often and why? How should the writing assignments look in computer-enhanced classrooms? And, for the purposes of this volume, what are the rules for electronic texts and how do we measure them fairly?

These are important questions to ponder as Composition moves deeper into its second decade of computer use and nears the second century of writing assessment. For a growing number of institutions, having technology available to the classroom is not in question in the same way it was just a few years ago. As a January 2003 *New York Times* article indicated, colleges and universities have invested heavily in creating digital classrooms (Marriott, 2003). Yet, ethical access is still a concern. First-year composition classes at some institutions are shut out of computer labs, whereas at other campuses the entire student body is using wireless networks for all classes. Ethical access in the cyberclassroom carries with it the expectation that "classroom borders are opened and new parties admitted into the rhetorical and social mix" (J. Porter, 1998, p. 3). But, as James Porter asked, what happens when student access buts up against campus computing policies (1998, p. 4)? Or, to extend Porter's argument, what happens when student discourse or e-texts clash with campus academic policies or codes of student behavior? What limits, if any, should instructors pose to curtail access? And if we decide to curtail access, how will our actions (and our students' actions) affect the assessment process?

James Porter, in discussing Lyotard's recognition that no one can escape obligation and judgment (J. Porter, 1998, p.53), pointed us toward a guiding direction for determining what ethical access is for these dual technologies. Writing instructors should take into account the "local we" (J. Porter, 1998, p. 53) in the shaping of a cyberclassroom's ethical access. The "local we" mirrors, in some sense, the standards that civic communities set for art, obscenity, and so on. In the "local we," there is a commitment that all members make to language and the technology used as well as to each other. This "local we" also influences the standards developed for writing assessment.

The "local we" extends access beyond the ability for students gaining time at the computer. As D. Porter (1999) stated, a significant but underdiscussed point in ethical access is how participants are welcomed in networked environments. For compositionists to generate ethical access to networked environments in the classroom, time must be spent considering how all students are included in discussions and online activities. There is plenty of anecdotal evidence to suggest that not all students feel welcomed on class listservs, blogs, and chat. These students either withdraw completely from discussion or decide to undermine discussions with reactionary points or underlife conversations. Neither situation benefits the "local we" or the instruction at hand. Yet, every student must feel a part of the ongoing writing in the internetworked discussions so his or her work can be judged as fairly as the next one's. That is why the entire class in relation to the programmatic guidelines needs to develop some type of protocol, or behavior, to pledge to work toward building a community in cyberspace.

Of course, ethical access extends to student ownership of the e-text, as outlined in chapter 3. It is at this point where an ethical assessment plan for online student writing should emerge. New questions arise for ethical assessment. For example, how much responsibility should students have in the evaluation of their e-texts? Where should this evaluation come from, the instructor only or additional external voices? How much value is the writing instructor to place on external visitors' comments about a student's class-based electronic text? How much privacy can be afforded student e-texts in networked class activities? At what point in the evaluation can or does the instructor's grading hand override or overwrite the student's e-text? These are all critical questions to pose as hot and cool technologies merge in the classroom. These questions, however, do not directly address "standards," the latest political and media buzzword connected to assessment. Far too often, standards are imposed on instructors and their classes from some external constituency. Following the "local we" concept, any and all standards are to be set by the community. In a cyberclassroom, this may include the students, the instructor, and the writing program administrator or the department and its policies.

Calling on the "local we" suggests that compositionists can have writing standards that foster an ethical assessment program for computer-enhanced classes. Tom Fox (1999), in proposing seven points for minority student populations to gain access in traditional writing classroom, offered several areas technorhetors can strive for to make access to computer and assessment technologies ethical in the cyberclass:

- Use writing and technology to investigate societal dysfunction—racism, sexism, homophobia, ableism, and so on in inter-networked spheres.
- Acknowledge that writing with technologies leads all writers into conflicts and contradictions at times, and every writer must search for ways to understand how these conflicts and contradictions can make us better writers for a global audience.
- Realize that technologies expose institutional inequities in the classroom, writing program, department, university, and stu-

dents' lives, and that compositionists should expect the interplay of these inequities to affect students' work.

- Discover that writing with technology illustrates how successful resistance occurs in the classroom and offers evidence for promise and possibilities in generating writing and thinking that is out of the box.
- Address the ways in which writing with technology is complex and requires students and instructors to take risks in their everyday practices.
- Demonstrate how writing with technologies shows that the past and present imbalances caused by social forces and that deny access can be overcome.

D. Porter (1999) pace Lyotard is right: None of us in the teaching of writing can escape our obligation to the institutions we teach for and remove ourselves from judging writing. However, compositionists can use the technologies we have before us to make the evaluations fair, just, and understandable to all involved. The point is to ensure that both instructors and students have sufficient access to and knowledge of these technologies before mandating their use in the classroom.

Chapter 7

Remediating Writing Assessment

I want to end this book on a hopeful note about technological convergence and its impact on writing assessment. Hope is exactly what writing instructors need in light of the politics of technology and of writing assessment in education. The reality is that these two technologies, computers and assessment, are here to stay in Composition. So too is the age of fast capitalism that drives not only the ways teachers teach writing and the ways in which teachers use computers in writing instruction but also the ways in which writing is viewed and assessed within education. Fast capitalism, with its need to generate rapid distribution of information and (intellectual) capital, also drives the push for more, better, faster, and efficient educational and evaluation models.

More college instructors have to become conscious of the growing number of external factors that influence the rationale behind the blending of technologies in the writing classroom. Most of these outside forces pressuring technological convergence in the composition classroom have little to do with learning and much to do with speed, efficiency, and political image. This is another harsh reality in higher education. Administrators feel the pressure from state legislatures that demand information on student outcomes, retention, attrition, and progress to make funding determinations. At times, faculty find the endless paper shuffling and document creation processes to be nothing more than academic exercises. In the end, from the faculty perspective, teaching lines are underfunded, technology purchases are tabled, and students never seem to have enough sections of the writing classes they need. Technological convergence looks more like bureaucratic boondoggle rather than educational initiatives at some institutions.

Still, there is much teaching faculty can do in their classrooms and in their writing programs to harness the power of technological convergence in ways that benefit student learning. Here is where hope enters into the discussion. Despite these external pressures, optimism exists for teachers to discover what they and their programs value about technological convergence in the writing classroom. The discussions these values can foster are the foci of this chapter. As with other campus or programmatic issues, our ability and willingness to construct dialogue and to articulate the importance of specific shared values related to convergence become central.

For hope to take hold, teachers must first realize that this is a critical time for the nexus of hot and cool technologies in writing pedagogy, because the terrain of ideas, information, skills, and strategies needed to be literate in society changes more quickly today than in previous eras. It is time for those of us involved in the teaching of writing, from K–12 teachers to college instructors to school and program administrators, to engage in redefining literacy practices that effectively synthesize these technologies in the writing classroom. The good news is that combining these technologies can take many forms in a writing program. This suggests that there are infinite ways to construct an assessment program that accounts for e-texts, as chapter 4 in this book outlines. What is of significant concern is for writing instructors to take notice of the need to incorporate these converging technologies. If we forget to pay attention, others can and will impose certain technologies on our teaching. These externally imposed technologies may not be appropriate for the types of writing curricula we imagine for our students. This is not fear speaking, but reality. Unwanted programmatic changes occur when faculty cannot or do not speak.

A few years ago in the *Atlantic Monthly*, Lester C. Thurow opined that "capitalism is a process of creative destruction. The new destroys the old …. The old patterns of powerful vested interests must be broken if the new is to exist, but those vested interests fight back. They are not willing to fade quietly into the pages of history" (1999, p. 62). Although Thurow was discussing the laws of radical suppression in capitalism, he might as well have been talking about Composition in the age of convergence between computer and assessment technologies. Both computers and assessment are by-products of capitalist thinking applied to education, in that the two reflect speed and efficiency in textual production. Yet one—computers—reflects the "new" and the other—assessment—the "old" technological means of writing production. When old and new forms collide in a context, one must give way to accommodate the other. In all likelihood, if Thurow's analysis based on the suppression model holds true, computer technology will subsume assessment technology in some way, as the new eventually overtakes the old in both capitalism and education. In a different venue, Jay David Bolter and Richard Grusin (2000) called this process "remediation."

The hope is that writing teachers begin to take greater interest in guiding the remediation process between computers and writing assessment. From what the field has seen with the rise of computerized grading software programs and the interest administrations have with such software, a forced remediated writing assessment program driven by speed, efficiency, and cost will benefit neither faculty nor students. An imposed assessment system is frequently a poor assessment system; generally, it is an assessment system that is cheap to implement and outdated in terms of authenticity. Yet these inexpensive assessment programs usually depend on powerful vested interests to promote the benefits of such systems. Writing teachers who are aware of these predesigned writing assessment software packages can develop stronger arguments against inauthentic computer-based writing evaluation. There are far better ways to meld computer usage with writing assessment than what compositionists have been offered.

COMING TO VALUE REMEDIATED WRITING ASSESSMENT

We all see remediated writing assessment looming on the horizon with Composition encouraging the use of e-portfolios in college writing classes. Growing numbers of colleges and universities seem intrigued by the use of e-portfolios for a culminating exit review of students' work. However, only in rare instances do carefully attended criteria exist for examining the e-portfolio. Most rubrics for e-portfolios look somewhat like the rubrics used for print-based portfolios, even though the texts within can vary dramatically. Many instructors find print-based criteria stifling when applied to genuine e-texts, because the guidelines do not account for important elements that readers and teachers value in the e-text. Frustration mounts for both teachers and students when writing assessment criteria are incompatible with the texts produced. This frustration can be compounded when complex e-texts are involved.

Not having clear evaluation models for e-texts makes assessment risky in that accountability is compromised, and the instructors' reviews become open to claims of subjectivity. Writing instruction frequently faces such claims, regardless of the medium in which the content is presented. However, because visual rhetoric and design are now included in the production of an e-text, a student's or a colleague's charge of disliking a particular piece based on visual appearance may be enough to make instructors second-guess their decisions. When the criteria for evaluation are weak, instructors expose themselves to negative commentary.

Worse yet is for writing teachers to ignore the call to establish some form of criteria for students' e-texts. Not having any guidelines in place at all implies that e-textual writing has no value in the writing classroom, for as White's saying goes, "We assess what we value in writing."

This is why it is important to for instructors to focus on what student proficiencies are valued in e-textual writing and how those competencies can be met through more sophisticated writing assessment models that embed continuous evaluation throughout the writing process. Because remediated writing assessment will have the ability to create voluminous learning traces, (e.g., the audit trails described in chapter 4), opportunities for summative and formative electronic writing assessment experiences exist.

Compositionists must discover what they value in an electronic text so the evaluation process becomes more refined than it currently is for many programs. If writing instructors do not discover ways to evaluate e-texts, evaluation models will be imposed on them. As many veteran teachers can attest, the old patterns of powerful vested interests connected to writing assessment do fight back, hence the rise of software programs, such as E-rater and the Intelligent Essay Assessor among others, that focus on electronic forms of normative holistic scoring driven by a preprogrammed algorithm. In these situations, it is not how the students fare on the writing test that matters; it is how quickly and efficiently the students' work can be processed that matters. Cost and time management of an assessment tool should not be the leading variables that drive how faculty measure student writing progress.

Drawing on the history of writing assessment in Composition, we can understand why software programmers selected a familiar evaluation model as the foundation for this type of software. Familiarity presumably breeds trust, in this case. The holistic scoring model has a long history in the teaching of writing. Composition specialists know about holistic rubrics for scoring essays. Writing teachers see and understand how the holistic scoring model can be used in print-based evaluation, and many believe the rubric can be transparently used to accommodate e-portfolios. Administrators find that the quantitative approach to normative scoring is comfortable and easy to disseminate. Students who are educated in elementary and secondary schools under the current push for standardized assessments fluently connect an abstract number to pass–fail. Even after the field's scholars presumed that normed scoring was a dying process, it is apparent that the normative approach to writing assessment will not fade quietly into Composition's history. Fast capitalism in higher education argues too well that this assessment model is quick, efficient, inexpensive, and seemingly objective.

The influence of fast capitalism in society, however, should also have us see the razing of one technological form by another happening much more rapidly than it has in the past. Because higher education is not immune to social forces, it is reasonable to think that newer forms of technology can and will become equal to, if not level with, older forms. This razing can be beneficial for writing assessment. Writing assessment models can be improved through advancing computer technologies, as I outlined in chapter 4. It is possible for writing teachers and their programs to escape normative writing assessment models for e-texts. The question that begs to be asked is, How soon can the field move from the imposition of these holistic software packages on writing programs and toward more effective electronic assessment models?

We know that technological change occurs swiftly in the Internet Age, as the period between the introduction of a new technology and the erasure of the old may be as short as just a few months. Remediation of older technology forms can happen repeatedly in the space of a year. Software assessment programs like E-rater and the Intelligent Essay Assessor may be relics before they truly begin to take hold because of the resistance many writing faculty have demonstrated toward the introduction of these programs. Most compositionists believe that it is important to note how students fare on their writing assignments; for them, evaluation is not something that can be driven by speed or efficiency. For now, the oppositional voice of compositionists has given many institutions pause before implementing computerized essay scoring software. However, if the field does not begin to consider alternative models for evaluating electronically produced writing, future resistance may be futile because the merging of computers and writing assessment will be co-opted by industries like ETS, Vantage, SCT, and others that can promise results at a fraction of the cost for maintaining faculty.

What makes the synergy between computer and assessment technologies so unusual compared with other forms of convergence is that there is a significant political and economic pull for both technologies in the rooms where decisions are made, and this tug of war slows down the remediation process. Although it appears that administrators and legislators agree that there need to be more technology and more accountability in teaching writing, there certainly is little agreement about implementation, costs to maintain, and success in measuring what students learned. All this impedes rapid technological convergence. One benefit of delayed progress is it offers time for solid Composition research to be conducted that can introduce new models for evaluating writing given the rise of computer technology.

My hope is that computerized writing assessment will evolve beyond the holistic model to better conform to teaching with technologies. That is the reason I wrote this book. We are seeing the beginning of this change in the continued call for greater e-portfolio use and in the creation of the Online Learning Record, TOPIC/ICON, and Dynamic Criteria Mapping. This is not to suggest that writing assessment will fade away, because it most likely will not without a major sea change in the legislative and administrative perspectives on accountability in the schools. Instead, teachers will lead the way for technological convergence by integrating best practices from each technology into a hybrid of something new. Therefore, Composition as a discipline must turn its thoughts toward deciding what assessment strategies work best for computer-based writing classrooms, because the decisions can mean the difference between faculty members constructing an assessment system that promotes powerful learning in networked environments or receiving more of the same, ill-suited conventional evaluation strategies ported over from present patterns of writing assessment. This is how the field can move toward a language that accommodates coherence in electronic text assessment.

What these newer electronic writing assessment genres suggest is that in convergence, writing assessment has to account for the types of transparency that occur when writing is publicly situated. Part of the new accountability in electronic writing assessment has to reflect the social and technical aspects as well as the aesthetic elements required for readers to appreciate the e-text before us. Consequently, a remediated form of writing assessment depends on a sense of immediacy that permits the rubric to "disappear." That is, the context for assessment is seamless from the process. In many ways, Bob Broad's Dynamic Criteria Mapping system (2003) opens the way for immediacy to occur in computer-focused writing assessment. Instead of rigidly following sets of descriptors made for paper texts, writing teachers can begin to account for the multiplicity of media and the students' facility with such media that exist to create e-texts; it is this context of how the writer selects and uses the appropriate media that frequently determines whether an electronic text is well received. The context and the media also allow instructors to observe changes in the student as author, how he or she responds rhetorically to these new contexts and media, the aesthetic determinations a writer must make, the growth in agency and ethos, and the development of parts to whole.

In a remediated understanding of writing assessment, compositionists must come to recognize that in an e-text various media simultaneously "honor, acknowledge, appropriate, and implicitly or explicitly attack one another" (Bolter & Grusin, 2002, p. 87). Therefore, writers have to adopt differing strategies to accommodate changes in the media. Assessment then emerges as an ongoing way to sanction or discourage specific strategies in context—through either academic, political, economic, or cultural forces—regarding the decisions a writer makes. Still, serious questions remain regarding how, or if, standards can be maintained in writing instruction given a remediated form of writing assessment through converged technologies.

REMEDIATION AND THE QUESTION OF STANDARDS

Few writing instructors have to go far before hearing some complaint about the current state of students' writing: E-mails from colleagues in other departments come across our screens asking us why students can't use appositives correctly; the daily paper has an op-ed piece from some think tank stating that Johnny, Jose, and Janiqua can't write well because of Instant Messenger; and the dentist asks why his kids don't write five-paragraph themes like he did when he was in school. Putting aside the old grammar game of incorrectly placing the comma in the legislative order so the world would be destroyed if the bill was enacted, listening to these various societal voices frequently makes a writing teacher wonder how civilization survived most people's wanton or wayward punctuation habits. Talk of lax writing standards abound everywhere, and the computer is blamed for much of students' real or perceived decline in written communication; the problem is not primarily with the computer, however. It is with how we perceive standards. Standards are representations that are subject to changes in language use and public literacy.

As Guenther Kress proposed, "In periods of great social flux, the degree of dynamism, the rate of change, can lead to a sense that there is no such stability to social-textual forms" (2003, p. 87). The rise of computer technology in writing has generated more social flux in language use, and it presents a far greater degree of linguistic dynamism than has occurred in earlier decades. The rate of change in introducing newer linguistic entries and discourse strategies in electronic communication has increased exponentially as well. Consequently, to those outside of writing or language studies, it may seem as though there are no standards in writing produced via networked environments. Some critics perceive, perhaps, that there is no hope for the written word now that computers have entered the fray.

As those who teach and write extensively in and for electronic communities realize, distinct standards exist for each online group. Discourse rules vary depending on who participates in the discussion. The community of users shapes the standards for language use and topic control. Standards that are violated tend to be sanctioned in some way by group members or moderators. What we learn from these communal practices is that writing standards adapt to shifts in both technology and culture. Standards are fluid and are formed by habituated practices that become internalized as ingrained representations. Those who lead the call concerning the demise of students' writing standards have internalized ingrained representations of print-based models of writing as being the standards for writing.

Yet, as we have learned from the varied practices of online writing communities, print-based standards are not necessarily the only standards that exist for composing a text.

To acknowledge the critics' concerns, computer technology does create a litany of questions for the current standards used in writing assessment. This, I think, is a positive move.

The field should regularly interrogate and challenge the standards used in writing assessment, perhaps even more so when technological changes affect the production of written texts. Clearly the computer has altered our writing habits and practices, and, at the moment, these activities are too new and too dynamic to establish ingrained representations of acceptable writing in networked environments. However, this flux should not prevent instructors from tracing these new habituated practices that shape written discourse in internetworked spaces. If anything, writing faculty need to be comparing and contrasting the types of texts and language produced for these various settings, because students need to have a linguistic awareness to write well in any format. While the claims of heterogeneity in language use and habituated practices exist in the literature on computers and writing, until teachers examine these changes, these assertions seem little more than lore. Without greater study, the call for heterogeneity in writing practices can be dismissed as a dodge against teaching "the basics." None of us are abdicating our responsibility to teach the fundamentals of writing—we're just in the process of determining what the basics are in this new technologically driven environment.

Most writing teachers realize that the homogenous understanding of writing standards that a few of our colleagues, some pundits, and the dentist, physician, butcher, and gas attendant have from their past experiences has morphed into something different. These differences should compel instructors to ask questions about the viability of standards for writing instruction. Although the use of computers contributes to these changes, the mere act of writing online is not the sole reason for the evolution of standards in writing assessment. We also must consider a more diverse student population, considerable governmental cutbacks in funding K–20 education, the increased public discussion of school accountability, and other regional factors in the talk of writing standards in addition to the rise of students' computer usage. We should also be wary of what I'll call "standards backlash"—the proposal that writing assessment needs to become more objective as more technology is introduced into the writing class.

Many proponents of traditional writing standards see hope for computer technology only when it blends with writing assessment in conventional ways. The current push for traditional assessment standards melding with computer technology in forms like the Intelligent Essay Assessor, E-rater, and other software programs provides a false sense of establishing objective standards that appear to be endlessly repeated across time and space. The developers' notion that these assessment programs are objective is specious: There are human agents programming the algorithms found within these assessment tools, ensuring that certain content is highlighted over other content, specific linguistic structures preferred over other forms. These agents compose the desired criteria and then have the machine control the processing. The result is not objective; rather, the result is a Fordist-style efficiency of mass grading student essays. This type of assessment is fine if learning is done in Henry Ford's Model T approach—one style, all in one tone. But as writing instructors have found with many writing assignments, learning does not occur in one style or all in one tone. This is particularly the case with students generating e-texts; reproducing a set format not only is undesirable but is a fiction exposed by the polyvocal and polyvalent nature of e-texts. The continual collection of various data forms will create a genuine objective data flow for evaluation—the student writing will exist in multiple formats for instructors to examine either summatively, formatively, or in both manners depending on the questions asked of the evaluation and the program's expectations.

A second problem with the current crop of computerized writing assessment programs is that no sense of immediacy exists in this type of writing assessment. An important thread to consider in this problem is how student learning will be affected, especially in the early stages of implementation, when students realize their work will be constantly recorded and subject to continual evaluation if the program or instructor so chooses.

Student writers will always be highly conscious of the assessment medium's presence. In the current crop of electronic writing assessment instruments, this is of particular concern, because the software makes the computer the focus of the assessment. As Negroponte (1995) observed, a strong interface design is transparent—that means students shouldn't realize they are involved in a writing test situation.

This overarching interface presence suggests that the software assessment programs are not authentic, and over time, it is plausible that students will try to write solely for the test or will devise systems to try to cheat the test. Cheating the test with these assessment software programs simply means students will discover that they only need to have the keywords presented in certain places and the remainder of the writing can be little more than babble. Or the writing can be vapid as long as the keywords or key concepts are presented in the text. Beating the machine in this manner relegates learning back to its days as rote instruction; students merely have to memorize the surface information and regurgitate it back on paper to pass the course. In short, reproduction outweighs production. Writing assessment becomes little more than refashioned indirect assessment.

However, as teaching writing with computers occurs with greater frequency, especially at the K–12 level where students become more familiar with various e-texts at a younger age, and teachers along with their students discover the multitude of possibilities that exist when writing e-texts, it will become increasingly more difficult to impose the types of control inherent in the Intelligent Essay Assessor and E-rater programs. The claims of objectivity in writing assessment that software programmers offer now will very likely be challenged, just as multiple-choice writing tests and holistic essay grading have been over the last three decades. And all of us will be at square one again, trying to determine what "the basics" are for evaluating e-texts in ways that demonstrate accountability.

Because there is no genuine objective method for writing assessment in either print-based or pixel-based composition, writing specialists have to work harder to explain to various constituencies why language standards have changed in the networked age and why writing assessment criteria have to change as well. One of the reasons why standards are changing in writing for electronic spaces connects to the power to control language. In the past, monks, academics, publishers, journalists, and schoolteachers controlled written language. It was they who dictated what proper usage was and how it looked on paper. These individuals were the audience, and many of us as students wrote for them and their approval. Their approval gave students' writing legitimacy. Their approval determined accountability.

Computer technology and its attendant offspring (laptops, cell phones, PDAs, wireless devices) inverted the power to control language and granted greater access to e-texts. Writers no longer need an outside authority to legitimate the printed word. Moreover, as many instructors have learned through our own experiences, these devices' constrained spaces require different objectives for the written word. Now, the goal with much of written language is to be quick, efficient, and timely. The receiver's acknowledgment of the message sent is often adequate enough to ensure legitimacy in a sent message.

Over time, the standards for writing assessment will most likely evolve to consider these three elements—quickness, efficiency of language, and timeliness of message content—as well as the electronic medium used to generate the e-text as part of "good" writing. Remediated writing assessment decades from now may be incredibly immediate and transparent in that a student could use a wireless device like a cell phone or PDA to write an e-text for a college entrance writing exam, if such a genre exists in the future (see Mike Palmquist's discussion regarding future PDA use in Hart-Davidson and Krause, 2004). More institutions are moving toward direct student placement for their writing programs, which reduces the need for a placement essay. Those colleges and universities that still require a writing exam have already moved to putting the college entrance essay or placement essay online, and as technology improves, it is not implausible to see wireless devices as part of this process. The immediacy of this writing context is that students will not perceive the e-text to be a writing test. Therefore, writing instructors should see more authentic student writing rather than the rigidly mimetic student essays now generated in response to testing situations. It is important to note that the student's composition may look more like the phonics-based writing we find on cell phones or BlackBerry transmitters today. That future text would reflect the real or perceived constraints of space that students realize exist in online writing. In many ways, future student writers might function like journalists on deadline, punching out assignments on BlackBerrys or cell phones and submitting them for review. That is why we must realize that language will evolve to conform to this new writing space. Eventually, as convergence becomes complete, an entrance composition written in texting language may be perfectly acceptable given the changing nature of the medium, the written word, and literacy standards. Part of remediated writing assessment will be for teachers to consider the medium in which the student submits an e-text for review. If language moves toward quick, efficient, and timely representations in constrained forms like a cell phone, then assessment must follow to some degree.

Another reason why assessment standards will change through convergence relates to the logic of the image rather than the logic of writing. As Kress explained, the book was organized and dominated by the logic of writing (2003). This logic extends to how information is organized or sequenced and shaped by the temporal, spatial, or sequential practices of writing that have been passed along generations. The logic of the image, however, is spatial–simultaneous (Kress, 2003). The logic of the image reorganizes how we write, because we now have to consider the arrangement of words on screen in relation to the surrounding images. No longer do words alone carry the text's content; the image shares in textual knowledge making. Words and images form two different modes of thinking and writing in electronic communication. Therefore, writers in these new textual environments have to think differently about the words and arrangements they use to communicate information. Writers must become multimodal (Kress, 2003), and remediated writing assessment means instructors have to begin to explore the potential for as well as the limitations of multimodality in writing and assessment.

The question of declining grammatical or mechanical standards exists on campuses now, and much of the blame goes to Instant Messenger programs or blogs or other electronic genres that function outside of the legitimating realm of the university. This question raises the relatively narrow understanding of language and technology that many people possess. Language, particularly orthography, is dynamic and highly subject to change. Frequently, language moves toward simplicity for all users. It may be that because of globalized communication via the Internet, American English is becoming more standardized to fit the wide variety of users in networked communication.

Writers who adopt the "texting language" found in cell phone or Instant Messenger usage may be displaying advanced literacy skills in that they are working with other discourse structures that will become widespread in the near future. It is plausible to think that in remediated writing assessment, a criterion for using discourse structures that reach out to the widest audience (right now, the texting language) would be preferred for online writing. This may require instructors to present a two-tiered language system, in which students learn the conventions of edited American English for print-based writing and the conventions for online communication (or "wired English").

The question of standards in remediated writing assessment, then, will be answered by repurposing what literacy standards are and the relations these standards have to writing assessment in networked environments. The process of repurposing writing standards simply means that instructors or programs must reconsider or revise the reasons for why student writers generate electronic texts. Any emerging standards will need to have a locus of authority and meaning in relation to the types of texts and writing our students complete for electronic communities. This suggests that a significant amount of unpacking the criteria must be done for writing instructors to discover what practices, what languages, and what level of visual rhetoric are needed so student writers can be successful in e-textual production.

Most likely, remediated standards will shift and be constructed by varying contexts and situations. The hope for remediated writing standards is that teachers will be able to better create a set of criteria that are fluid and flexible enough to accommodate a range of student produced e-texts without sacrificing critical values that an instructor or a program may have regarding writing. In the process, these shifting standards will offer new understandings of literacy and new consequences for students not meeting criteria set for e-texts. In the best possible scenario, remediated writing assessment will be like ubiquitous computing—the standards will be embedded into all forms of electronic writing to the degree that students and instructors find it to be part of everyday experiences.

A cautionary note remains in writing assessment, whether in its present stage or in a remediated form. There are dishonest students, instructors, administrators, and legislators who undermine evaluation through various dodgy uses of the data or input corruption. Larger discussions need to happen with remediated writing assessment to find ways that prevent misuse of these large database collections of student information without violating students' rights to textual ownership, hindering student and instructor performance, and misrepresenting the curriculum.

TOWARD A SYNCRETIC UNDERSTANDING
OF TECHNOLOGIES IN THE WRITING CLASSROOM

With the convergence of technologies in writing instruction, teachers have to be aware that remediating writing assessment through the growing use of computers in the writing classroom can lead us toward syncreticism. Syncretics, the blending together of differing traditions or schools of thought—in this case assessment and networked writing environments—offers writing teachers a richer, more varied understanding of how technology can be beneficial for composition pedagogy. The culture and practices that arise from syncreticism allow us to identify the workable elements of the older culture (assessment) that share similarities with elements in the newer culture (computers). As those elements are identified and discussed over time and across various conditions, an environment emerges that fuses "what works" into a set of practices and pedagogical habits.

Because writing instructors and their programs are in the middle of technological convergence, any prescriptive offering to come to the rescue seems narrow at best and dogmatic at worst. Schools and colleges across America and the world are in very different stages as far as in-place infrastructure and assessment philosophy. Instructors and their programs are not now, nor may they ever be, at a place where "one size fits all" for the convergence of computer and assessment technologies in their institutions.

As I proposed earlier in this book, the most promising and syncretic avenue for remediated writing assessment comes from teachers developing models of deep assessment that account not just for content and mechanics but also for techne, aesthetics or visual rhetoric, and genre recognition. In deep assessment, standards carried over from earlier forms of writing assessment can be blended with the ideas we value in teaching with computers. In a syncretic system, deep assessment becomes a type of "assessment as design" in which evaluators create criteria that are flexible and accountable in response to the course level taught and the range of student ability.

A syncretic understanding of remediated writing assessment generated through convergence offers the hope that the field moves toward ubiquitous deep assessment. This offers a type of evaluation that integrates into our daily experiences and habituated practices. Composition is not at that point yet, but ubiquitous deep assessment is an attainable goal. The foundations are in place. Now moving forward demands all instructors and program administrators to reconceptualize the substance and the business of converging two seemingly disparate technologies into the existing values of their campuses.

This book is not meant to state what writing teachers can and cannot do with writing assessment and computers in their classrooms. Because infrastructures, budgets, and missions vary greatly across institutions, any prescriptions would be ill-fitting solutions to the problem. Rather, the issues raised throughout this work have been set forth to generate larger discussions about how instructors and their programs move forward to balance the weight of two equally demanding technologies in their teaching. The conversations put forward in this book have been designed to motivate writing teachers to articulate what they value in e-texts, writing assessment, and internetworked writing experiences to find the answers to the problems that exist in their home institutions. This suggests that syncretism seems to be the most workable method to point writing teachers in the directions that they and the field need to head.

Syncretic thinking about technological convergence in Composition indicates that we won't necessarily scrap older ideas in favor of newer ones. Syncretic thinking also implies that there are ways to blend seemingly disparate traditions and habitual practices. There is no doubt that syncretic thinking about the convergence of computers and writing assessment will continually challenge us to revisit and rearticulate what we value about each technology and what we value when the two technologies are blended into our pedagogy. The hope is that compositionists discover what mix of the old and new technologies works best for their programs before external pressures force a remediated writing assessment plan that fits no one's interests.

References

Allison, L., Bryant, L., & Hourigan M. (1997). *Grading in the post-process classroom.* Portsmouth, NH: Heinemann/Boynton-Cook.

Alter, J. (1999, September 20). Bridging the digital divide. *Newsweek.* Retrieved September 20, 1999, from http://www.newsweek.com

Amerin, A., & Berliner, D. (2002). High-stakes testing, uncertainty, and student learning. Education Policy Analysis Archives. Retrieved from <http://epaa. asu.edu/epaa/v10n18/

Annas, P. (2004). *New words: A postrevolutionary dictionary.* Retrieved from www.wpunj.edu/radteach/rt-def.html

Apple, M. (2003). *The state and the politics of knowledge.* New York: RoutledgeFalmer.

Apple, M. (2001). *Educating the "right" way.* New York: RoutledgeFalmer.

Apple, M. (2000). *Official knowledge.* New York: Routledge.

Austin, J. L. (1962). *How to do things with words.* London: Oxford University Press.

Baron, D. (1998, November 20). When professors get A's and machines get F's. *The Chronicle of Higher Education,* A56.

Batson, T. (2002, December 20). The electronic portfolio boom: What's it all about? *Syllabus Magazine,* 16(14), 4.

Baudrillard, J. (1990). *America.* (C. Turner, Trans.). New York: Verso.

Belanoff, P., & Dickson, M. (1991). *Portfolios: Process and product.* Portsmouth, NH: Boynton/Cook.

Berlin, J. A. (1987). *Rhetoric and reality: Writing instruction in American colleges, 1900–1985.* Carbondale: Southern Illinois University Press.

Black, L., Daiker, D., Sommers, J., & Stygall, G. (1992). *New directions in portfolio assessment: Reflective practice, critical theory and large-scale scoring.* Portsmouth, NH: Boynton/Cook.

Blair, K., & Takayoshi, P. (1997). Reflections in reading and evaluating electronic portfolios. In K. B. Yancey & I. Weiser (Eds.), *Situating portfolios: Four perspectives* (pp. 357–369). Logan: Utah State University Press.

Bolter, J. D., & Grusin, R. (2002). *Remediation: Understanding new media.* Cambridge, MA: MIT Press.

Brice Heath, S. (1990). The fourth vision: Literate language at work. In A. A. Lunsford, H. Moglen, & J. Slevin (Eds.), *The Right to Literacy* (pp. 288–306). New York: Modern Language Association.

Broad, B. (2003). *What we really value: Beyond rubrics in teaching and assessing writing.* Logan: Utah State University Press.

Bruffee, K. (1993). *Collaborative learning: Higher education, interdependence, and the authority of knowledge.* Baltimore: Johns Hopkins University Press.

Charney, D. (1994). The effect of hypertext of processes of reading and writing. In S. Hilligoss & C. Selfe (Eds.), *Literacy and Computers* (pp. 238–263). New York: Modern Language Association.

Connors, R. J. (1996). The abolition debate in composition: A short history. In L. Z. Bloom, D. A. Daiker, & E. M. White (Eds.), *Composition in the twenty-first century: Crisis and change.* Carbondale: Southern Illinois University Press.

Day, M. (2000). Teachers at the crossroads: Evaluating teaching in electronic environments. *Computers and Composition, 17*(1), 31–40.

Deleuze, G., & Guattari, F. (1987). *A thousand plateaus.* Minneapolis: University of Minnesota Press.

Derrida, J. (1988). *Limited Inc.* Evanston, IL: Northwestern University Press.

Duin, A. H., & Hansen, C. (1994). Reading and writing on computer networks as social construction and social interaction. In. S. Hilligoss & C. Selfe (Eds.), *Literacy and Computers* (pp. 89–112). New York: Modern Language Association.

Dupuis, A. (1997). *Trading in futures: Why markets in education don't work.* Philadelphia: Open University Press.

Educational Testing Service (ETS). (1999). GMAT testing begins. Retrieved from http://www.ets.org <http://www.ets.org

Elbow, P. (1996). *Embracing contraries.* New York: Oxford University Press.

Engell, J., & Dangerfield, A. (1998, May–June). Humanities in the age of money. *Harvard Magazine.* Retrieved from <http://www.harvard magazine.com/issues/mj98/mj98issue.html

Faigley, L., Cherry, R., & Jolliffe, D. (1986). *Assessing writers' knowledge and processes of composing.* Hoboken, NJ. Ablex.

Farris, C., & Anson, C. M. (1998). *Under construction: Working at the intersections of composition theory, research, and practice.* Logan: Utah State University Press.

Feenberg, A. (1991). *Critical theory of technology.* London: Oxford University Press.

Fidler, R. (1997). *Mediamorphosis: Understanding new media.* Thousand Oaks, CA: Pine Forge Press.

Forbes, C. (1996). Cowriting, overwriting, and overriding in portfolio land online. *Computers and Composition, 13*(2), 195–205.

Former U of Nebraska student sues over posting of personal essay. (1998, February 20). *The Chronicle of Higher Education.* Retrieved from http://www. chronicle.com

Fox, T. (1999). *Defending access: A critique of standards in higher education.* Portsmouth, NH: Heinemann/Boynton-Cook.

Freire, P. (1993). The banking model of education. In D. Bartholomae & A. Petrosky (Eds.), *Ways of Reading*. Boston: Bedford Books.

Fu, D. (2000). The contested "I": Portfolios and cultural values. In B. S. Sunstein & J. H. Lovell (Eds.), *The portfolio standard: How students show us what they know and are able to do*. Portsmouth, NH: Heinemann/Boynton-Cook.

Fukuyama, F. (1995). *Trust: The social virtues and the creation of prosperity*. New York: Free Press.

Gilster, P. (1997). *Digital literacy*. Hoboken, NJ: Wiley.

Gronlund, N. (1998). *How to make achievement tests and assessments*. New York: Longman.

Grossberg, L., Wartella, E., & Whitney, D. C. (1998). *MediaMaking*. Thousand Oaks, CA: Sage.

Haas, C. (1996). *Writing technology: Studies on the materiality of literacy*. Mahwah, NJ: Lawrence Erlbaum Associates.

Habermas, J. (1991). *The structural transformation of the public sphere: An inquiry into a category of bourgois society*. Cambridge, MA: MIT Press.

Hart-Davidson, B., & Krause, S. D. (2004). RE: The future of computers and writing: A multivocal textumentary. *Computers and Composition, 21*, 147–160.

Herrington, A., & Moran, C. (2001). What happens when machines read our students' writing? *College English, 63*(4). Retrieved from http://www.ncte. org/pubs/journals/ce/articles/109744.html

Hesse, D. (1999). Saving a place for essayistic literacy. In G. Hawisher & C. Selfe (Eds.), *Passions, politics, and 21st century technologies* (pp. 34–48). Logan: Utah State University Press and Urbana, IL: NCTE.

Hillocks, G. (2002). *The testing trap: How state assessments control learning*. New York: Teachers Press.

Himley, M. (1991). *Shared territory: Understanding children's writing as works*. New York: Oxford University Press.

Hopkins, K. (1998). *Educational and psychological measurement and evaluation* (8th ed.). New York: Allyn & Bacon.

Howard, T. (1997). *A rhetoric of electronic communities*. Greenwich, CT: Ablex.

Huntley, J., & Latchaw, J. (1998). The seven Cs of interactive design. In J. R. Galin & J. Latchaw (Eds.), *The dialogic classroom: Teachers integrating computer technology, pedagogy, and research* (pp. 106–130). Urbana, IL: National Council of Teachers of English.

Huot, B., & Williamson, M. (1993). *Validating holistic scoring for writing assessment: Theoretical and empirical foundations*. Cresskill, NJ: Hampton Press.

Huot, B. (1996). Computers and assessment: Understanding two technologies. *Computers and Composition, 13*(2), 231–243.

Huot, B., & Williamson, M. (1998). What differences the differences make: Theoretical and epistemological differences in writing assessment practice. In C. Farris & C. M. Anson (Eds.), *Under construction: Working at the intersections of composition theory, research, and practice*. Logan: Utah State University Press.

Huot, B. (2002). *Re-articulating writing assessment*. Logan: Utah State University Press.

Jaworski, A. (1993). *The power of silence: Social and pragmatic perspectives.* Thousand Oaks, CA: Sage.

Johnson-Eilola, J. (1994). Reading and writing in hypertext: Vertigo and euphoria. In S. Hilligoss & C. Selfe (Eds.), *Literacy and Computers* (pp. 195–219). New York: Modern Language Association.

Joyce, M. (2001). *Othermindedness: The emergence of network culture.* Ann Arbor: University of Michigan Press.

Kemp, F. O. (2002). TOPIC/ICON. Retrieved from http://English.ttu.edu: 5555/manual

Kress, G. (1994). *Writing the future.* Urbana, IL: National Council of Teachers of English.

Kress, G. (1995). *Making signs and making subjects: The English curriculum and social futures.* London: Institute of Education.

Kress, G. (1998). Visual and verbal modes of representation in electronically mediated communication: The potentials of new forms of text. In I. Snyder & M. Joyce (Eds.), *Page to screen* (pp. 53–79). New York: Routledge.

Kress, G. (1999). Genre and the changing contexts for English language arts. *Language Arts, 32*(2), 185–196.

Kress, G. (2003). *Literacy in the new media age.* New York: Routledge.

Lauer, J., & Asher, J. W. (1988). *Composition research: Empirical designs.* New York: Oxford University Press.

Lemann, N. (1995a, September). The great sorting. *Atlantic Monthly.* Retrieved from http://www.theatlanticmonthly.com

Lemann, N. (1995b, August). The structure of success in America. *Atlantic Monthly.* Retrieved rom http://www.theatlanticmonthly.com

Leslie, L., & Jett-Simpson, M. (1997). *Authentic literacy assessment.* New York: Addison-Wesley/Longman.

Light, R. (1999). *The Harvard assessment seminars: Explorations with students and faculty about teaching, learning, and student life* (3rd Report). Boston: Harvard University.

Marriott, M. (2003, January 12). Beyond the blackboard. *New York Times.* Education Life supplement. Retrieved from http://www.nytimes.com

Maykut, P., & Morehouse, R. (1994). *Beginning qualitative research.* Oxford, UK: Macmillan.

McLuhan, M. (1964). *Understanding media: The extensions of man.* New York: New American Library, Times Mirror.

Messick, S. (1989). Validity. In R. L. Linn (Ed.), *Educational measurement* (3rd ed., pp. 72–102). New York: Macmillian.

Moss, P. A. (1992). Shifting conceptions of validity in educational measurement: Implications for performance assessment. *Review of Educational Research, 62*(3), 229–258.

Murray, D. (1991, June). Exploring webpage literacy in language learning. Address given to FEELTA Pac 5 Conference. Retrieved from http://www.dvgu.ru/rus/partner/education/feelta/pac5/about_Murray_ pr.html

Nachmias, C., & Nachmias, D. (1981). *Research methods in the social sciences.* (2nd ed.). New York: St. Martin's Press.

National Council of Teachers of English. (2001). *NCTE statement on writing assessment.* Retrieved from http://www.ncte.org

National Telecommunications and Information Administration (NTIA). (2000, October 16). *Americans in the information age falling through the net*. Retrieved from http://www.ntia.doc.gov/ntiahome/digitaldivide

Negroponte, N. (1995). *Being digital*. New York: Vintage.

Newell, A. (1986). The models are broken. *University of Pittsburgh Law Review, 47*, 1023–1035.

Nunberg, G. (1996). *The future of the book*. Berkeley: University of California Press.

Ott, C. (1999, May 25). Essay questions. *Salon*. Retrieved from http://www.salon.com/tech/feature/1999/05/25/computer_grading

Pailliotet, A. W. (1999). *Intermediality*. Boulder, CO: Westview Press.

Patel, S. (1996). Graduate students' ownership and attribution rights in intellectual property. *Indiana Law Journal, 72*(2). Retrieved from http://law.indiana.edu/ilj/v71/no2/patel.html

Peeples, T., & Hart-Davidson, B. (1997). Grading the "subject": Questions of expertise and evaluation. In L. Allison, L. Bryant, & M. Hourigan (Eds.), *Grading in the post-process classroom: From theory to practice*. Portsmouth, NH: Heinemann/Boynton-Cook.

Penrod, D. (1994). *Architextural practices: The essay as architecture, the essay as architext*. Unpublished doctoral dissertation, Syracuse University, Syracuse, NY.

Porter, D. (1996). *Internet culture*. New York: Routledge.

Porter, J. (1998). *Rhetorical ethics and internetworked writing*. Greenwich, CT: Ablex.

Press, E., & Washburn, J. (2000, March). The kept university. *Atlantic Monthly, 285*(3), 39, 14.

Rheingold, H. (1991). *Virtual reality*. New York: Simon & Schuster.

Rheingold, H. (2003). *Smart mobs*. New York: Perseus.

Saffo, P. (1992). Paul Saffo and the 30-year rule. *Design World, 24*, 18–23.

Schlacter, E. (1997). The intellectual property renaissance in cyberspace: Why copyright law could be unimportant on the internet. *12 Berkeley Tech Law Journal*. Retrieved from http://cyber.law.harvard.edu/metaschool/fisher/library.html

Schuster, C. (1992). Climbing the Slippery Slope of Assessment. In L. Black, D. A. Daiker, J. Sommers, & G. Stygall (Eds.), *New directions in portfolio assessment: Reflective practice, critical theory, and large-scale scoring* (pp. 314–324). Portsmouth, NH: Heinemann/Boynton-Cook.

Selfe, C. (1997). *Technology and literacy: A story about not paying attention*. Paper presented at the College Composition and Communication Conference, Chicago.

Selfe, C. (1999, February). Technology and literacy: A story about not paying attention. *College Composition and Communication, 50*(3), 411–436.

Selfe, C., & Hilligoss, S. (1994). *Literacy and computers*. New York: Modern Language Association.

Selzer, J. (1996). *Kenneth Burke in Greenwich Village: Conversing with the moderns 1915–1931*. Madison: University of Wisconsin Press.

Snyder, I., & Joyce, M. (1998). *From page to screen*. New York: Routledge.

Stallings, W. D. (1997). *Distance education*. Englewood Cliffs, NJ: Prentice-Hall.

Sutherland, K. (1998). *The electronic text: Investigations in method and theory.* Oxford, UK: Clarendon Press.

Sweedler-Brown, C. O. (1991, Fall). Computers and assessment: The effect of typing versus handwriting on the holistic scoring of essays. *Research and Teaching in Developmental Education, 8*(1). Retrieved from http://www.rit. edu/~jwsldc/NYCLSA/RTDE/contents/8-1.html

Syverson, M., & Slatin, J. (1999). *The online learning record.* Retrieved from http://www.cwrl.utexas.edu/%7Esyverson/olr/contents.html

Takayoshi, P. (1996). The shape of electronic writing: Evaluating and assessing computer-assisted writing processes and products. *Computers and Composition, 13*(2), 245–258.

Thompson, C. (1999, July–August). New word order. *Lingua Franca.* Retrieved from http://www.linguafranca.com/9907/nwo.html. Lingua Franca 09.5

Thurow, L. C. (1999, June). Building wealth. *The Atlantic Monthly, 283*(6), 57, 10.

Tornow, J. (1997). *Link/age: Composing in the online classroom.* Logan: Utah State University Press.

Turkle, S. (1999). *Life on screen: Identity in the age of the internet.* New York: Touchstone.

Tyner, K. (1997). *Literacy in a digital world: Teaching and learning in the age of information.* Mahwah, NJ: Lawrence Erlbaum Associates.

Wenglinsky, H. (2002). How schools matter: The link between teacher classroom practices and student academic performance. *Education Policy Analysis Archives, 10*(12). Retrieved from http://epaa.asu.edu/epaa/v10n12/

White, E. (1994). *Teaching and assessing writing.* (2nd ed.). San Francisco: Jossey Bass.

Wickliff, G. (1997). A hypertext authoring course, portfolio assessment, and diversity. In K. B. Yancey & I. Weiser (Eds.), *Situating portfolios: Four perspectives* (pp. 322–337). Logan: Utah State University Press.

Wilhelm, J. (2000). Curatorial collections: Cross-curricular design portfolios. In B. S. Sunstein & J. H. Lovell (Eds.), *The portfolio standard: How students show us what they know and are able to do.* Portsmouth, NH: Heinemann/Boynton-Cook.

Wimmer, R. D., & Dominick, J. R. (1997). *Mass media research: An introduction.* (5th ed.). Thompson Wadsworth.

Winston, B. (1998). How are media born and developed? In J. Downing, A. Mohammadi, & A. Sreberny-Mohammadi (Eds.), *Questioning the media: A critical introduction* (pp. 277–292). Thousand Oaks, CA: Sage.

Yancey, K. B. (1999, February). Looking back as we look forward: Historicizing writing assessment. *College Composition and Communication, 50,* 483–504.

Yancey, K. B. (2004). Looking for sources of coherence in a fragmented world: Notes toward a new assessment design. *Computers and Composition, 21,* 89–102.

Yancey, K. B., & Weiser, I. (1997). *Situating portfolios: Four perspectives.* Logan: Utah State University Press.

Zak, F., & Weaver, C. (1998). *Theory and practice of grading writing: Problems and possibilities.* Albany: State University of New York Press.

Author Index

Subject Index